MATHEMATICAL
BRAIN BENDERS

MATHEMATICAL BRAIN BENDERS

2nd Miscellany of Puzzles

STEPHEN BARR

DOVER PUBLICATIONS, INC.
NEW YORK

Published in Canada by General Publishing Company, Ltd., 30 Lesmill Road, Don Mills, Toronto, Ontario.
Published in the United Kingdom by Constable and Company, Ltd., 10 Orange Street, London WC2H 7EG.

This Dover edition, first published in 1982, is an unabridged and corrected republication of the work originally published in 1969 by The Macmillan Company of New York under the title *2nd Miscellany of Puzzles— Mathematical and Otherwise.*

Manufactured in the United States of America
Dover Publications, Inc.
180 Varick Street
New York, N.Y. 10014

Library of Congress Cataloging in Publication Data

Barr, Stephen.
    Mathematical brain benders.

    Reprint. Originally published: 2nd miscellany of puzzles.   New York : Macmillan, 1969.
    1. Puzzles.   2. Mathematical recreations.   I. Title.
GV1493.B28   1982   793.73   81-19527
ISBN 0-486-24260-9   AACR2

Add another hue unto the rainbow . . .
>> *Shakespeare*

We subtract faith and fallacy from fact . . .
>> *Samuel Hoffenstein*

Be fruitful and multiply . . .
>> *Genesis*

Round numbers are always false . . .
>> *Samuel Johnson*

Vicious circle . . .
>> *George Du Maurier*

Straight down the crooked lane and all around the square . . .
>> *Thomas Hood*

Every cubic inch of space is a miracle . . .
>> *Walt Whitman*

The god delights in an odd number . . .
>> *Virgil*

Euclid alone has looked on beauty bare . . .
>> *Edna St. Vincent Millay*

Measure your mind's height by the shade it casts . . .
>> *Browning*

Gaul is all divided in parts three . . .
>> *Caesar*

Is 5 . . .
>> *e. e. cummings*

CONTENTS

PUZZLES

A SUBMISCELLANY OF SHORT PUZZLES, MORE OR LESS FROM EVERYDAY LIFE

MATHEMATICAL
BRAIN BENDERS

PUZZLES

1

ROLLERS

Figure 1 shows the side view of two equal wheels between two parallel rails; if there is no slipping, the wheels can roll either way and still maintain their vertical relative positions. The same would be true if they were spheres and the horizontal lines were planes.

If, however, the top sphere were much larger than the lower (Fig. 2), and they were pushed to one side, which would go ahead of which?

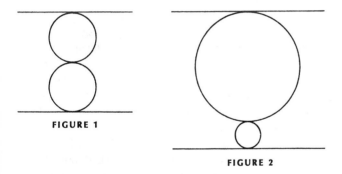

FIGURE 1

FIGURE 2

2

OWL'S EGGS

On Owl Island the eggs are spherical. Two men were about to boil some, when one of the men, a mathematical crank, said, "I wonder if it takes more water to cover a big egg than a small one. I mean in *this* pot," he added, when he saw his friend, a mathematical noncrank, was about to say that it would depend on the size of the pot. The pot was an exact cylinder, 4 in. in diameter.

The noncrank said, "Obviously 'to cover' means the level of the water is to be at the high point of the egg (Fig. 1), and if the egg was an ostrich egg there wouldn't be very much room for water around it (Fig. 2). Then again if it was an ant's egg you'd only need a teaspoon or less (Fig. 3)." Having agreed on this, they made separate measurements of the pot, and separate calculations. The crank was as good at figuring as the noncrank, but he believed that $\pi = 3$. The noncrank knew better, but he used a ruler for measuring that was 1% off, while the crank's ruler was exact. Each worked out the radius of egg that took the most water to cover it in their pot. Which was most nearly right?

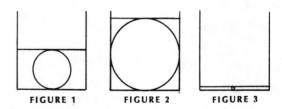

FIGURE 1　　　FIGURE 2　　　FIGURE 3

3

CONICAL HELIX

There is a helical line around a right-circular cone, measuring 2 along the slanting radius, PA, and with bottom diameter 1. The curve starts tangent to the base at P, makes one circuit, and ends vertically at A, the apex—to which it is thus radial. There is a radial line, P'A, diametrically opposite to P, and P'A intersects the curve exactly halfway along the length of the curve, and at an angle of 45° at I.

What is the simplest expression which will precisely define and describe the curve?

Question 2

Where does the φ proportion come into it? *

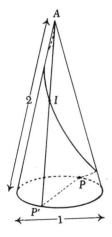
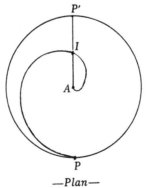

—Plan—
(P brought around to the front)

* For a definition of φ, see Puzzle 27.

4

THE OWL ISLAND FLAG

Having settled the egg-covering problem, a third islander said it gave him an idea for a flag—"to put over the door," he explained. "The door is 4 ft. wide and the design will be a red square on a white ground, but only at the sides." He made a sketch (see figure). "It's the same problem as your stupid egg-and-water one (Puzzle 2); how big should the red square be to give the greatest amount of white on the sides? Width of flag to be 4 ft. of course."

"It's not the same problem at all," replied a friend. "In this case you don't need calculus to get the answer."

Without calculus, what value of h gives the maximum of white?

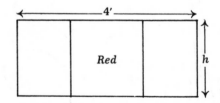

5

PSEUDO-MOEBIUS STRIP

Make two paper strips, one to be 1 in. x 11 in. (*A*), and the other 1 in. x 10 in. (*B*), and join as shown. Before attaching *B*—a cylinder—*A* has two sides, two edges and two half-twists. The final form will have two sides and one edge.

If we now cut along the dotted lines, what will be the result? Give number of sides, edges, and twists. Answer must be got without cutting along dotted line.

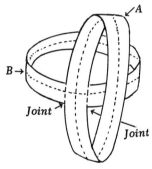

Question 2

This can be done without clairvoyance. If, after joining the ends of *A* together and attaching *x* to *x'*, we were to move *y* 4 in. along in the direction of the arrow (see figure), and *then* cut along the dotted lines, how would it affect the final form?

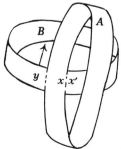

23

6

THE BUTLER AND THE CRUMBS

A maid was about to wipe off a rectangular table, measuring 4 ft. by 8 ft., when the butler, a methodical type, took over. "System's what you need, my gal!" he said. They both had short arms and could only reach 2 ft. with the dust-cloth, so he decided to get all the crumbs together at the center point, *C*, on one long side. He walked along the opposite side, *AB*, pushing all the crumbs as far as he could directly toward *C*, and then did the same at each end, finally going to the other long side to pull them toward the dustpan. When he had done so, the maid complained. What did she say and why?

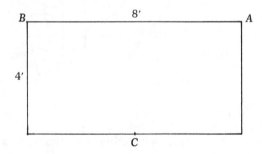

7

THE THREE CLOCKS

I wake up late on Sunday and find a note from my wife: "I had to go out—be back for dinner. Today we change the clocks because of daylight saving—but I can't remember if we put them ahead or back an hour, so I set one of our three clocks ahead, and another back. I couldn't find the third one. I know they were all correct and fully wound last night."

I have no watch, radio, TV, phone, or sundial—or neighbors—and no way of telling time. I find *one* clock, and from it I can deduce the right time. How?

8

SLIT STRIPS

If a strip of paper is joined into an untwisted (cylindrical) loop, and then cut lengthwise along the center line, it comes apart into two similar, but narrower, loops. If given a half-twist before joining—thus becoming a Moebius strip, with one side and one edge—and cut lengthwise it remains in one piece, a longer loop with four half-twists. A loop with two half-twists has two sides and two edges, like the first, and when cut lengthwise it also comes apart into two loops, but they are linked. Also they are twisted the same way as the one they were cut from (Fig. 1).

If we cut a slit in the strip before joining (dotted line, Fig. 1), and push the end through it, and then join (Fig. 2) and cut as before (by extending the slit), what will the result be? Give number of loops and twists, and whether linked, with reasons.

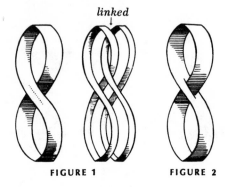

linked

FIGURE 1   FIGURE 2

Figure 1 shows two arbitrary forms, differing only in their lower halves; one is the mirror image of the other. If, instead of making a slit as we did before, for the strip to pass through, we make part of the strip wider and with a hole (Fig. 2), the part that goes through can be turned either way, or neither, as shown in the figure. We now combine this method of intersection with the lower halves of the forms in Fig. 1; the results are shown in Fig. 3.

If we now cut them both along their center lines, considering the holes as part of the cut, how will the resultant forms differ from each other?

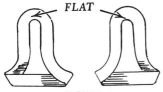

FIGURE 1

FIGURE 2

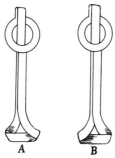

FIGURE 3

9

THE POT ON THE CROSSPIECES

A large cylindrical pot has been set over an open fire on crosspieces of metal bars, at right angles and with sharp upper edges marked in inches out from the center, for some forgotten reason.

The pot has been pushed to a precarious position (see figure), and from where we are we can see that the circular bottom just intersects the bars at the 6-, 8-, and 15-in. marks.

What is the diameter of the pot?

Question 2

Later the pot is replaced by another less than a third its size. It intersects the crosspieces at the 1-in. mark on one crosspiece, and the 2- and 3-in. marks on the other. Apart from its diameter, what can be said about it?

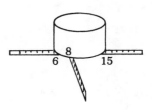

FOR SCRABBLE PLAYERS

On the assumption that only Scrabble players will try this puzzle, we have left out the rules. If the reader is an exception, we suggest buying this excellent game. We have, however, given rules that apply to what words are allowable—a matter of style.

Question

In a single play, and under what circumstances,

4		1			4			1			4
	2			3			3			2	
		2			1		1			2	
1			2			1			2		1
				2				2			
	3		1		3		3			3	
		1			1	1			1		
4		1			✳			1			4
	1			1		1			1		
	3			3			3			3	
		2						2			
1		2			1			2			1
	2			1	1			2			
	2		3			3			2		
4		1		4			1			4	

The Board*

* The star is the middle square, which is a double word score; 1 means double letter score; 2 means double word score; 3 means triple letter score; 4 means triple word score.

Continued on next page

10 Continued

with what word can a player score at least 1,000 points?

Give the whole word pattern leading to this score, so that the whole could have been reasonably (if somewhat rashly), arrived at, keeping strictly to the rules. For example, when a foreign word is not generally considered to have been anglicized, even though it is often used in English, most dictionaries give it, but prefixed by parallel bars: || flaneur [F.]. When a foreign word is given without the bars it may be used. The single word asked above, however, must be English and well known.

11

AREA OF ROOF

There is a 10-ft.-wide, cubical shed with a pyramidal roof; when seen from far enough to show no perspective distortion, and from a point opposite the center of a side, one sees a square surmounted by an equilateral triangle, as shown here. Without paper or pencil, give the actual area of the roof (time limit, one minute).

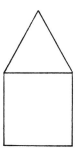

12

PAPER-FOLDING

There are two rectangles of paper, measuring 1 x 2, and 1 x 3, in separate rooms. Without bringing them together, in how few folds can one indicate equal angles (other than 45°) in each rectangle? Nothing but folding and creasing is allowed, and we have no measuring devices.

13

THE TWO PYRAMIDS

An explorer in Tabasco, Mexico, came back to camp to announce the discovery of two Mayan pyramids in the jungle. "One has a square base, and the other a triangular base," he said. "But the interesting thing is that all the edges of both are exactly the same length."

One of his partners said, "There's a record of them; they were built of the bricks taken from a still older monument, which had gone out of fashion—you know how those things are. All the records say is that the old one, like your discoveries, had all its edges equal, that all three monuments were solid, and that all the brick from the old one was used in the new ones. Oh, I nearly forgot: the old one wasn't a pyramid, but some other simple geometrical form."

A mathematical member of the team asked, "What is the length of the edges of the pyramids?" When he was told, he said, "Then I know the height of the old monument."

What was it, and what was its shape?

14

THE MAN WHO GAVE UP SMOKING

A man was looking sadly at a full package of cigarettes from which he had torn the end (Fig. 1), and wondered how many could be removed without loosening any others. So he tried rearranging them. Obviously if C was missing, A could slide down, and D up. Or if A was missing, C could slide from between B and D. But the absence of B left things firm.

He soon found that the arrangement in Fig. 2 was no good because the group EFGH could rotate as a whole. He was never able to pack in less than fifteen firmly, but he did find an arrangement with five cigarettes in each of the three rows.

Continued on next page

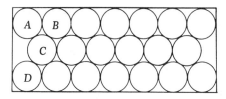

FIGURE 1

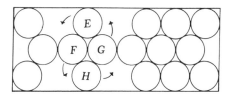

FIGURE 2

Question 1

What was it?

The coin collector from across the hall came in and suggested experimenting with coins on the table, in a rectangular frame. "It's more accurate," he said, and added, "I wonder why they don't make square packages." But he soon saw that hexagonal packing would never be square (Fig. 3), because the horizontal would be multiples of the radius of the cigarettes (or coins), but the verticals always involved $\sqrt{3}$. His wife pointed out that they could be packed square (Fig. 4). "And they wouldn't have to put so many cigarettes in for the size of the package," she added. "Sixteen in an eight-radii square, and if it's done at an angle (dotted line, Fig. 4), you'd only get twelve in, and the square would be only slightly smaller." She looked pensive. "I wonder how *big* a square you could pack with twenty, and still have them held rigid. . . ."

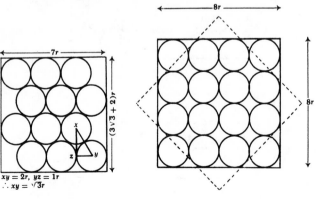

$xy = 2r,\ yz = 1r$
$\therefore xy = \sqrt{3}r$

FIGURE 3   **FIGURE 4**

The coin collector got to work, and after a while he said, "With the diagonal packing you can get eighteen tightly in a square just over 9 x 9 (Fig. 5), but twenty, hmmm. . . ." Finally he had it. "And the square's slightly *larger* than the last one!"

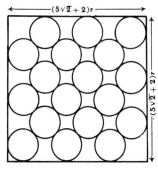

←————— $(5\sqrt{2}+2)r$ —————→

$(5\sqrt{2}+2)r$

FIGURE 5

Question 2

Give the arrangement.

Then the nonsmoker said, "I can do it with only sixteen circles! And the square is *still* larger."

Continued on next page

14 Continued

Question 3

Give the arrangement.

Everyone admired it, but after a moment the coin collector's wife said, "Oh dear—I'm afraid it won't do. It's not rigid." She turned out to be right.

Question 4

Explain why.

"To return to the hexagonal problem," the coin collector said, "it is actually possible to pack six in a square—not too difficult to do—but the question is, how big is the square? I happen to like geometrical constructions, so I want to solve it that way."

Question 5

Give the arrangement and geometrical construction for finding the largest square. Explain all answers in detail.

15

TETRAHEDRON ANGLES

Any or all of the faces of a tetrahedron may be right triangles, with the right angles distributed in various ways. Obviously no two right angles can be in the same face, and, for example, in the figure, if three right angles are at the same vertex, there cannot be a fourth one, because it would make two of the edges parallel.

What are the restrictions in the case of a tetrahedron which has only three right angles, with two at one apex, and the third at another? Give proof.

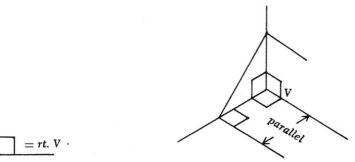

$\boxed{} = rt.\ \text{V} \cdot$

V is the farthest vertex

16

HYPOCLOIDS

When a small circle, A, rolls around the inside of a larger one, B, a point, P, on the small one traces a series of arcs which form a hypocycloid curve, C. If the circles are commensurable, e.g., as shown here (Fig. 1), where the diameter of A is one-sixth of the diameter of B, the hypocycloid joins up with itself.

In Fig. 2 the inner circle is larger; in fact five-sixths the size of the outer one, and rotates the same way as circle A in Fig. 1.

In what respect, if at all and to the eye of a nonmathematician, would the path traced by point P′ differ most noticeably from the path of P in Fig. 1?

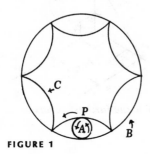

FIGURE 1

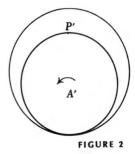

FIGURE 2

17

SQUARES ON A CIRCLE

Equal squares are placed symmetrically around a circle so that their inner corners touch it; their diagonals are on radii and their contiguous corners touch one another, as in the diagram.

Obviously there cannot be less than five squares, because with four their inner corners would meet at a point. With five the radius, r, of the circle is incommensurable with the side of a square.

Question

What is the smallest number of squares with side $= 1$, which will give a rational value for r? Prove without algebra.*

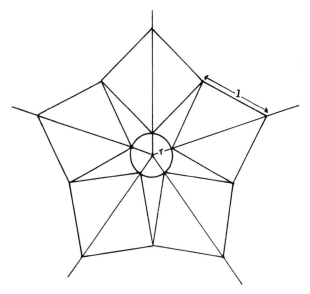

* This restriction does not apply to showing that a *smaller* number of squares gives an irrational value for r; only to the proof that the correct smallest number gives a rational value.

18

THREE COINS

Three coins lying flat on a table all touch one another, and their centers form a right triangle; give their sizes in the smallest possible whole numbers. No paper and pencil; time limit, one minute.

19

TWO COINS

A coin collector had a table with an exactly circular hole in it, where long ago had been an inkwell. He had two pure gold coins of the same thickness; the larger exactly fitted the hole, and the smaller one, when slid gradually over the hole, tipped into it when its edge reached the center of the hole. The larger coin weighed 6 oz. (Troy); what was the weight of the smaller?

20

THE COIN COLLECTOR'S NIGHTMARE

The coin collector was experimenting with coins of various sizes, putting them flat in groups of three to see what angles their centers made. He had two 1-in.-radius coins on the table, touching, when his wife asked him, "What size coin would make a right angle with them?"

"That's easy," he said, and drew Fig. 1. "Root two minus one."

"No, I don't mean with their centers," she said. "I mean with their outsides, like this." She pushed the coins symmetrically into the corner of an inverted box lid (Fig. 2). "Now, how big a coin will fit into the corner? And don't give me any more algebra; just geometry." He nodded.

"That was geometry I was using before," he added. "I suppose you mean a geometrical construction." When she came down for breakfast next morning he had the answer.

What was the construction, using compass and straight edge only?

FIGURE 1

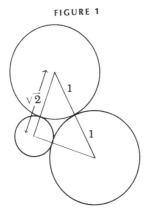

FIGURE 2

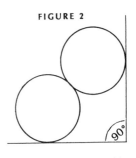

21

THE HI-Φ SET

"I bet you," said the coin collector's wife, "that you can't arrange a set of six equal coins so they make a ϕ proportion somewhere." (For the definition of ϕ, see Puzzle 27.) "I mean," she went on, when he frowned, "you can line them up with a right angle, like the corner of this box lid we were using several pages back."

He shook his head. "You do it," he said.

She did. How? The proportion must appear as two definitely determined distances or lengths, e.g., from one tangent point to another, or the distance between two coins from edge to edge; but no arrangement can be made except by contact of one coin with another, or alignment against the two straight edges, which are at right angles—the box lid mentioned above.

22

CRYPTARITHMETIC

A cryptarithm is a sum in arithmetic, worked out, but given in letters which stand for digits, the same letter always standing for the same digit, and positive unless otherwise designated. The one here is a problem in subtraction, as shown by the minus sign, but each letter stands for a positive digit. Some cryptarithms are tricky, and contain hidden clues.

$$
\begin{array}{r}
\text{ROME} \\
-\ \text{SUM} \\
\hline
\text{RUSE}
\end{array}
$$

(The number represented by "– SUM" is to be subtracted from "ROME.")

23

ORIGAMETRY

In origami, the art of paper-folding, we are allowed no instruments of any kind. It is assumed that a fold is straight, and that length and angle can be bisected by folding. If we start with a paper rectangle, we can fold it across twice, giving three creases (vertical in Fig. 1), that divide the area into four equal parts. Let us assume that we can trisect the other dimension, and make the two horizontal creases shown. We have now divided the whole into twelve equal areas. By choosing appropriate sections of these creases, we can now demarcate any fraction of the whole area, in which the denominator is 12. For example, Fig. 2 shows in heavy lines one-, five-, seven-, and eleven-twelfths. The question is how we can, with only three creases, subdivide a rectangle so that we can demarcate any fraction with denominator 24? (If one fold makes two creases they both count.)

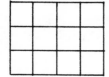

FIGURE 1

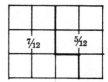

FIGURE 2

24

THE HAUBERK

Medieval chain armor was usually made like Fig. 1. As can be seen, every ring was connected with four others around it, and actually linked with each. An armorer from Pilsen arrived at the castle of an English lord and said they were doing it all wrong.

"In Bohemia we don't believe in linking the rings," he said, holding up the arrangement shown in Fig. 2. "These three are connected but not linked."

The lord was impressed. "You mean you can make an entire hauberk this way?" (A hauberk is a tunic of chain mail.)

"Certainly," replied the armorer.

He proceeded to do so, and when finished, no rings were linked together. How were they arranged?*

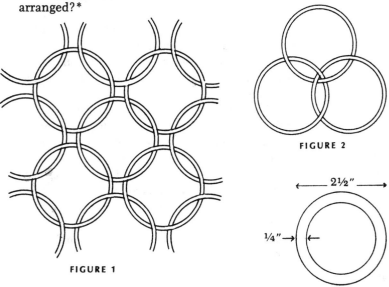

FIGURE 2

FIGURE 1

2½"

¼"

FIGURE 3

* Experimental models are best if made of paper, flat, and about 2½-in. outside diameter, and not more than ¼ in. wide (Fig. 3).

25

MORE ORIGAMETRY

Starting with a square sheet of paper, fold it to produce a square having three-fourths its area. Only five folds are allowed.

26

UNIQUE PARTS OF LETTERS

Is there any part of any letter of the alphabet that is unique? That is, a segment of a letter, such as the cross stroke of A, which cannot be found in the corresponding place in any other letter—which of course is *not* true of the cross stroke of A, because it could be a part of the cross stroke of H.

We confine ourselves to block capitals, without serifs or differences of line thickness, or such details, so that the little stroke on a Q can be got from part of the lower right side of A. In that case we would have to move it slightly to the left, which is allowed, but vertical distance from the line base must be the same. We can take part of an element, but not alter its size, so that the loop of P will not make the loop of D.

27

FOR Φ FANS

The ratio between the parts of a line, divided so that the lesser is to the greater as the greater is to the whole, is called the Golden Section, the *Divina proporzione*, or in some geometry books, the Extreme and Mean proportion. It is represented by the Greek letter ϕ (phi), and we derive it from this equation (see figure):

$$a : b = a + b : a, \therefore \frac{a}{a+b} = \frac{b}{a}, \text{ If } b = 1, a = \frac{\sqrt{5}+1}{2} = \phi, (1.618034\ldots)$$

In the following equation, what does x equal?

$$\phi^{\left(\phi^x - \frac{x-1}{\phi}\right)} - \frac{1}{\phi} = x$$

28

THE TRUCK GARDENS

In Geometria everybody grows vegetables for a living. The law says that all truck gardens must have the same area as the plan of the dwelling they go with, and that all dwellings—including single-family houses, apartment houses, and the apartments themselves—must be cubical. Thus if you lived in an apartment, your garden would have the area of the square plan of your apartment.

An entrepreneur, Geo. T. Hales, decided to build an eight-family apartment house next to and touching his single house. The houses were bordering on a huge rectangular field at its corner, which the zoning law forbade building *on*—but it could be used for gardens. Hales had a square garden in front of his house (Fig. 1).

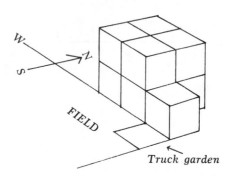

Truck garden

FIGURE 1

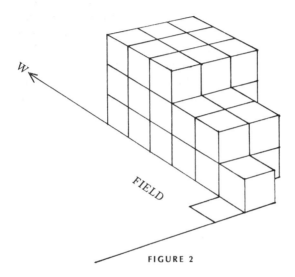

FIGURE 2

His profits were so high that he was able to build another, 3 x 3 x 3-unit, apartment house (for 27 families) beyond to the west (Fig. 2). In each case every family wanted a garden plot out on the field, and each succeeding year a new, cubical, apartment house was added; always to the west, and one unit wider than the last. What was the simplest way to plan the garden plots, with an unlimited field?

29

Φ ORIGAMETRY

According to the more Procrustean * Origamians, we may only fold, never cut. However, they do start out with a square, which is usually cut. But it can be made from a ragged-edged piece of paper in five folds—so we shall make another (imaginary) fold, and start with a 1 x 2 rectangle. The problem is to produce the ϕ ratio by folding the rectangle only twice. The ratio can be between any definitive points or other demarcations we end up with.

* This may seem an odd word for an Origamian, since Procrustes did a lot of cutting. Also stretching, for which reason he described himself as the first topologist.

30

THE COCKEYED KITE

A boy was making a kite; he had two pieces of bamboo for the ribs, and two pieces of silk. The former were 4 ft. long, and he joined them at right angles. One piece of silk was an isosceles triangle, ABC, 20 x 20 x 15 in., and the other was a scrap from which he intended to cut the upper triangle, as in the pattern (Fig. 1). He also planned to string wires along the outer edges, but being a bit absent-minded, he attached the big triangle sideways (Fig. 2). He strung the wire along the edges AB and BC, and continued with the first 9-in. length, CD, and then found that the second 9-in. section of wire wouldn't reach across DA. His young brother, who was very quick at arithmetic, said, "See? It won't reach—you put the first triangle on sideways! Bet you don't know how long DA is." The kitemaker immediately began figuring. He was slow at arithmetic but more mathematical, and beat his brother to it. What does DA equal and how did he do it?

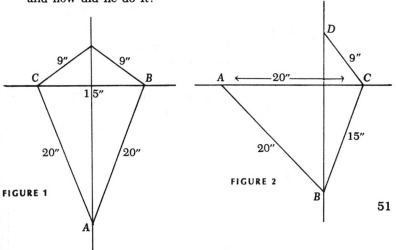

FIGURE 1

FIGURE 2

51

31

MORE Φ ORIGAMETRY

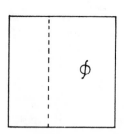

With no more than four folds, produce a crease in a square piece of paper—the dotted line in the figure—which marks off a ϕ proportion rectangle. Prove.

32

THE BOOKMARK

A professor wanted to mark a page in a book by folding down a corner, but when the book was closed, it didn't show. Also he wanted to mark the book so he could find it. He experimented with folding the page so that it projected *beyond* the edges of the others, but without tearing or pulling it loose. (The covers, which usually project slightly, will be ignored.)

Having found the method of folding which gave the maximum projection—in distance, not area—he saw that one of the outer corners of the folded page was exactly on one of the edges of the other pages. If the height of the book is 1, how far did the page project?

33

SNOW ON THE ROOF

During the night, snow had fallen, and the professor went out to the tool shed to get the shovel. "Wonder how deep it is," he said. "It's very sticky, so it won't do any sliding on the roof."

"Why don't you take the folding rule and measure it?" his wife said.

He came back shortly, looking vexed. "I took the foot rule by mistake," he said, "and the snow's a lot deeper than a foot; still, I was able to measure its thickness on the east slope of the shed roof—they're both at 45°—because when the snow comes down at an angle it's thicker on one side than the other. It was 10 in. Then I found an old rake handle, and I was able to measure with a pencil mark on it that the snow was exactly the same thickness on the deep side—west—as it is on level ground. Incidentally, the wind was steady from the west all night. The radio said so."

"Well why don't you measure where the mark on the handle is with the foot rule? Then we'll know how much snow we got."

"Didn't think of it. Left them both in the shed. Anyway, it doesn't matter—I can work it out with elementary geometry. Just the thing for measuring the elements. Ha, ha."

What was the thickness, and how did he do it? ("Thickness," of course, means at right angles to the roof, or the ground.)

34

DRAFTING PUZZLE

A draftsman has no instruments but a compass, and a sheet of paper which he does not fold, and which can be bought at *any* stationer's. How does he establish and mark the six vertices of a regular hexagon with only *one* placing of the point of the compass?

35

THE PSYCHEDELIC CUBE

Optical illusion is not new in the arts; any realistic picture in perspective is an optical illusion. Parenthetically, such pictures are abstractions—of a three-dimensional reality—whereas so-called abstractions, not being *of* anything, would be more correctly termed concretes, or Aldens, since they speak for themselves. A perspective representation is the projection by lines converging to a point of a three-dimensional object onto a plane. It differs from orthogonal projection in that the latter uses parallel lines. In both cases a cone, shown at an angle, gives an image which is an ellipse with two lines (see figure). The illusion succeeds; we see a cone.

Our problem here is to carry the process one stage further: To make a three-dimensional model (of cardboard) which, when viewed at the correct angle, and with one eye, will give the illusion of having a different form, in this case a cube, seen from the corner. The required model will thus be the projection in perspective of a cube onto a *different* three-dimensional form, but the *simplest*. (Describe the projection in detail.)

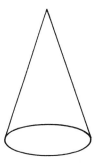

36

CONSTRUCTION PROBLEM

The figure shows the plan of a projected building to house two identical storage bins, between
which will be a staircase of constant width, a.
For structural reasons corners C and D must
lie on the diagonal AB, a supporting beam.
Given the dimensions AE and AF, show the simplest geometrical construction that gives the
dimensions of the bins.

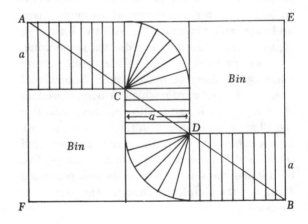

37

A WALK IN A FIELD

A man is standing in a flat field, 1 rd. (more than 5 yds.), due east of a post, and facing north. He walks straight north until he is directly northeast of the post; then—always in a straight line—he walks northwest until he is directly north of the post; then west until he is northwest of it; then southwest until he is west of it; and so on, in a kind of segmented spiral. When he is again due east of the post, how many rods is he from it? Give the formula, with d = distance from post in rods, and n = number of segments walked.

Question 2

If he walked one more segment, and was northeast of the post again, n would be 9, and $2^9 = 512$. To find the root of 512 he would need a book of tables; give a formula that can be memorized, and with which he could calculate his distance from the post as accurately as he could *with* tables. We assume he can memorize a number of, say, 8 digits, and has pencil and paper for the simple arithmetic needed.

38

MORE DIAGONALS

At the advice of the builders of the storage building of Puzzle 36, it was decided to put reinforcing beams under the diagonals of each bin, *ED* and *CF;* but the angles *EDB* and *ACF* must be right angles. Under these circumstances, what would be the ratio of the length of the building, *l,* to its width?

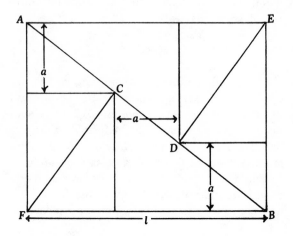

39

SHORT PROOF (CUT CUBE)

What two planes, passing through edges and/or vertices of a cube, divide one of its dimensions into three equal parts?

The proof must be as short as possible, and the figure to which it refers must be a drawing of the cube (transparent, if necessary) with no more than three added lines. The cube may be shown at any convenient angle. To explain and describe the figure you may make a subsidiary diagram, but the proof must refer only to the former.

40

WORD-CHANGING

There is a parlor game in which one word is changed to another of equal length, one letter at a time, so that at each stage we have a word. For example, CAT to DOG:

CAT
COT
DOT
DOG

Letters may not be transposed; all words must be English or British or their variants as given in standard dictionaries, but not requiring capitalization. Plurals are allowed, as are verb-derived forms such as RUNNER, etc. Compounds needing hyphens are not allowed. The object is to make the change in as few steps as possible; the example above is in the minimum, three, for all three letters had to be changed.

Question 1

Can you change ASK to WHY in seven steps?

Question 2

Now can you change SPRING to WINTER, in eighteen steps?

POLYHEDRAL MODEL

A piece of cardboard shaped as shown in the figure is creased along the six lines of the hexagon; three alternate triangles, x, are folded forward to meet at a point, and the remaining three triangles are folded back to meet at another point behind. The result is a twelve-faced, semiregular polyhedron with alternate faces missing, but with all its edges and vertices.

Question 1

What is the dihedral angle between any alternate pair of faces, i.e., any two of the cardboard faces that have a common vertex?

Question 2

If we now imagine that the six existing faces are extended in their planes to meet one another, but with their present vertices remaining stationary, what is the simplest description of the resultant form?

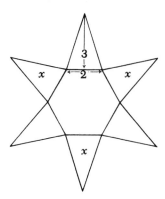

42

DIHEDRAL ANGLES

The solution to the previous puzzles depended on recognizing the given form as part of a cube; we now ask for the determination of the dihedral angle between a given pair of triangles in the form without reference to the cube, and proved by elementary geometry. The figure shows that we use only part of the original stellated regular hexagon, and the two triangles, *AEB* and *CFD:* What is the dihedral angle between the triangles when bent up so that *E* and *F* coincide?

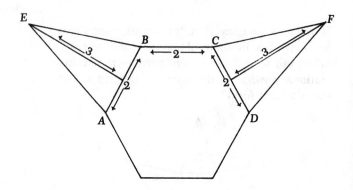

43

CHEESE WEDGES

Two ladies were going to make toasted cheese sandwiches, and found the cheese was in the form of little right-angled wedges (Fig. 1).

"They're exactly the wrong shape," said Mrs. V. "We have to cut them up so they lie flat. I make vertical cuts and arrange the triangles to fit the bread. One wedge just does for a sandwich."

The other, Mrs. H., said, "I prefer to cut them horizontally (Fig. 2) into slices that can be fitted with the slanting edges together, and they work out just right for me, too." She was talking to their mathematical friend, Mrs. M., so she added, "By a funny coincidence the uncut wedges, which are all alike, have exactly the same proportions in plan, when they are lying flat with the short side vertical, as the rectangles of bread, but too small. Mrs. V. makes almost four times as many cuts as I do, but we can both arrange our slices so they exactly fit the bread, which is trimmed to rectangles. I arrange mine in one row."

Mrs. M. didn't look at the cheese wedges or the bread. "Tell me one thing," she said, "has the bread the more or less normal proportions? Because if so I can tell you the exact relative dimensions of the uncut wedges."

What were they?

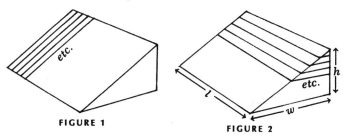

FIGURE 1   **FIGURE 2**

63

44

THE POISONED GLASS*

"Mathematicians are curious birds," said the police commissioner to his wife. "You see, we had all those partly filled glasses lined up in rows on a table in the hotel's kitchen. Only one contained poison, and we wanted to know which one before we searched for fingerprints. Our laboratory could test the liquid in each glass, but the tests take time and money, and we wanted to make as few of them as possible. So we phoned the university and they sent over a mathematics professor to help us. He counted the glasses, smiled and said:

" 'Pick any glass you want, Commissioner. We'll test it first.'

" 'But won't that waste a test?' I asked.

" 'Not *quite*, and I like to gamble,' he said. 'It's part of the best procedure. We can test one glass first. It doesn't matter which one.' "

"How many glasses had to be tested?" the commissioner's wife asked.

"I don't remember. Somewhere between one and two hundred."

What was the exact number of glasses? It is assumed that any number of glasses can be tested simultaneously by taking a small sample of liquid from each, mixing the samples, and making a single test of the mixture.

*My thanks to Martin Gardner for permission to use his version—much improved—of my puzzle The Poisoned Glass, which appeared in *Scientific American*.

45

TO COVER A CIRCLE

A man wanted to cover the biggest possible circle with a paper rectangle, 1 x 2 in. Flat, it would cover a 1-in.-diameter circle, but folded as in the figure it covered a slightly larger one, and he was trying to work out the maximum when his Japanese friend Suzi Origami came in. "I know you disapprove of cutting," he said, "so I was trying to do it by folding. If I increase the angle α it allows more room at the points of contact, C, but the little gap at V gets bigger and cuts into the circle. If I decrease α, the C's move in, so I'll have to use calculus."

"Not at all," replied Suzi. "The exact shape can be arrived at by folding only. The proof will need some calculation, but. . . . Oh, I forgot; it's only true if you make a symmetrical arrangement like yours, with only one fold, which goes through the center point, O. In my artless symmetrical way I'm quite good at avoiding calculus."

How did she do it?

This figure shows the method they both used, and with the correct value for α to get the desired result. (The dotted arc shows the advantage gained.)

Within what limits does the above apply, when we vary l?

Question 2

What is unusual or interesting about the triangle ADC in the original case, with $l = 2$?

Question 3

46

PURE-ORIGAMI SOLUTION*

The next evening Suzi went to a paper-folding bee in the Village, and took her friend Lillian aside and told her about the problem of covering the circle (Puzzle 45). "I didn't want to confuse the issue with our rules or predilections," she explained, "so it wasn't until afterwards that I worked out how to do it *without* knowing the proportions of the paper rectangle. Once you know the method you don't have to calculate anything; it's pure origami and it only takes eight folds."

The method makes use of the relationships proved in Puzzle 45, but no measurements (with a ruler) have to be made, and it works for any rectangle, diophantine or otherwise, between the limits given: 1 by 1.865 . . . and 1 by 2.915 . . . What is the method?

---

* This puzzle is for Origamians who don't want to bother with a lot of math. Just skim over Puzzle 45, and keep in mind the final single-fold shape, and the all-important equation $y = \frac{1}{8}$, and the fact that the fold must be symmetrical, i.e, the fold goes through the center point of the rectangular paper.

47

THE FLAT PAN

A man has a bowl that holds a little more than a pint, and a flat rectangular straight-sided pan that holds exactly a pint. The figure shows its proportions. He wants to put exactly one-third of a pint of water into the bowl, but he has no other means of measuring anything. He has a supply of water and an ordinary kitchen table with an exactly level surface. How does he do it?

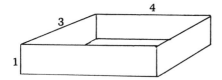

48

THE SIAMESE MOEBIUS STRIP

Take a strip of paper and cut two longitudinal slits (Fig. 1). Bring the upper pair of ends together and join with a half-twist so that *A* joins *A'*, and *B* joins *B'*. Then do the same with the lower, but twisting in the opposite direction. The result will be like Fig. 2. If it is then cut along the dotted line—also shown in the unjoined strip (Fig. 3)—what is the result? Give number of pieces, sides, edges, and twists, and explain. The model may be made, but do not cut along the dotted line; work out the answer by reasoning.

| A | | B' |
| B | | A' |

Slit   *Slit*

FIGURE 1

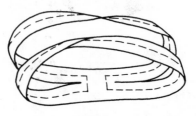

FIGURE 2

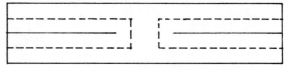

FIGURE 3

49

Excluding zero, the nine digits are written down in any arbitrary order (first line, Fig. 1). Under these we write the ordinal numbers that give the positions of the digits in the first line. Thus we start with 7, because in the first line 1 is the seventh number; then we write the number that gives the position of 2, in this case 6, and so on. We shall call this operation X. If we now apply the operation to the second line (Fig. 1), it gives the first line again. This will always be true no matter what the order of the first line is.

In some cases all three lines are the same, for example when the first is a list of the digits in their natural or reversed order.

Figure 2 gives two sequences of the nine digits. The second could have been produced from the first by operation X, but both were in fact produced by a completely different operation—and separately. To be quite precise, the operation was not exactly the same in the two cases (Fig. 2), but similar. What was it?

FIGURE 1	FIGURE 2
9 4 7 3 6 2 1 5 8	3 6 9 2 5 8 1 4 7
7 6 4 2 8 5 3 9 1	7 4 1 8 5 2 9 6 3

50

MINIMUM AREA

Draw a rectilinear figure of minimum area, with the following properties:

(1) Its sides are equal;

(2) Its angles are all right angles (reentrant or not);

(3) Its perimeter equals that of a given square with side $= s$;

(4) It is a closed figure whose sides do not touch or cross;

(5) It is quadrisymmetrical; that is, symmetrical about two axes at right angles.

For example, Fig. 1 does not follow (3) for its perimeter $= \frac{20}{3}s$, instead of $4s$. If we reduce its size the perimeter can be made to match. However, Fig. 1 does not follow (4) for its sides touch or cross at x. If we open x (Fig. 2) to conform to (4), sides y will be longer than sides z.

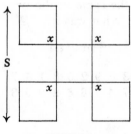

FIGURE 1

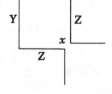

FIGURE 2

51

COCYCLIC POINTS

Five paper rectangles—one with a corner torn off—and seven paper disks have been tossed on a table. They lie as shown in the figure. Each corner of a rectangle and each spot where edges intersect marks a point. The problem is to find three sets of four cocyclic points: four points that can be shown to lie on a circle. For example, the corners of rectangle R are such a set, because the corners of any rectangle lie on a circle. What are the other two sets?

52

THE TILTED CARTON

Assume that we have a very thin, almost weight-less milk carton, which is flat-topped and exactly square in plan. Its height is twice its width. When full it can be tilted until its center, C, is vertically above the bottom edge, B, before tipping (Fig. 1).

If it were half-full, and tilted to the same position as before (Fig. 2), it is obvious that its new center of gravity would be to the right of the vertical axis, AB; so we know it can be

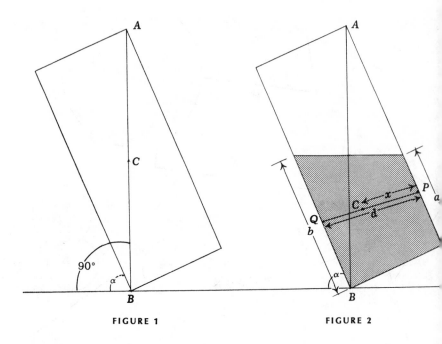

FIGURE 1   FIGURE 2

tilted further before tipping. However, if the carton were empty—and we do not ignore its infinitesimal weight—its center of gravity would be where it was when full. In Fig. 2 we can find the center of gravity (this time ignoring the weight of the carton) from the trapezoid (shaded) by the formula

$$x = \frac{d}{3} \cdot \frac{a + 2b}{a + b}$$

where P and Q are the midpoints of the parallel sides a and b, d is the median, C the center of gravity, and x the distance PC. When the carton is tilted to bring C vertically above B, the trapezoid changes, because the level of the milk remains horizontal, and thus C moves along PQ. Ignoring the carton's weight, what is the amount of milk, in terms of the dimensions of the carton, which allows the greatest tilting, and what will α be?

53

TOPOLOGY PUZZLE

The figure shows a piece of paper that by cutting, twisting and rejoining, has been given one side, two edges, and two holes, if we do not count the outer edge as a hole, as we should if it were distorted topologically into a sphere, as shown.

The problem is to make a model that has two sides, two edges, and seven holes, the latter being counted in the same way as above. Give any general rule that applies.

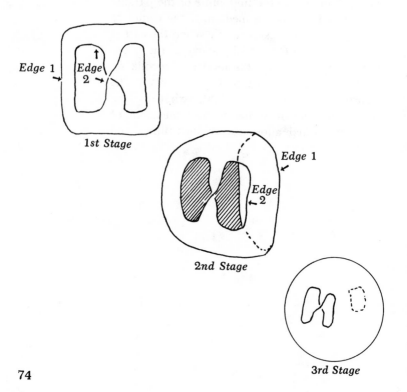

1st Stage

2nd Stage

3rd Stage

54

THE VANADIUM STEEL CLOTHESLINE

The professor's neighbor, Mrs. M, had hung out the wash with the greatest of zeal, on a tightly stretched line of vanadium steel; running corner to corner it's very genteel, but the wind it has blown it away—right into the professor's yard. It was winter, and the cloth had all frozen stiff, and he was trying to figure out what the odd shapes were, when Mrs. M stuck her head over the fence.

"I'm so sorry," she said, "those are my tablecloths. I always hang them corner to corner—that way they seem to dry quicker" (Fig. 1). Then she noticed that he was folding the corners in (Fig. 2).

Continued on next page

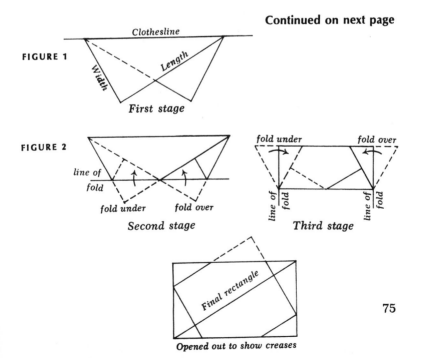

FIGURE 1

Clothesline

Width · Length

First stage

FIGURE 2

line of fold

fold under · fold over

Second stage

fold under · fold over

line of fold · line of fold

Third stage

Final rectangle

Opened out to show creases

75

54

"Yes," said he, "no matter what the proportions of the original rectangles were, folding them this way makes new rectangles. Smaller, and with different proportions, of course."

"What," said Mrs. M, "is the proportion between the proportions?"

"I don't know yet—I'll have to work it out. Let's see. . . ."

"I made one of those tablecloths myself," she said, "It's ϕ proportion—I wonder if you can tell which it is from the proportion of the folded rectangle."

The professor said, "While I'm working on that, see if you can tell me why the red one is the same proportion when folded as it was before."

"All right," she said. "But remember, no calculus!"

Explain how they both succeeded. The clothesline may be considered as a straight line, being of tightly stretched vanadium steel wire.

55

In this puzzle no drawings or experiments with any objects are allowed.

We have ten square cards measuring respectively 10, 9, 8, etc., down to 1 in. The even numbered ones are black; the others, white. If we put the 10-in. black one down, and then on it the 9-in. white one, not centered but pushed to the *top left* corner (Fig. 1); then on that put the 8-in. one to the *bottom left* of the 9-in. one (Fig. 2); then the next smaller to the *bottom right*, and so on, with the positions rotating—going inward counterclockwise—what pattern results in black and white when they are all down?

Describe fully.

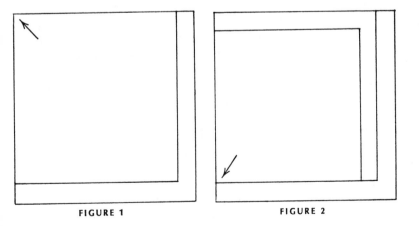

FIGURE 1   FIGURE 2

56

THE BALANCE

FIGURE 1

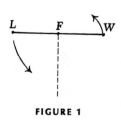

FIGURE 2

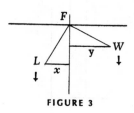

FIGURE 3

Figure 1 shows a diagram of a simple balance, in which the load to be weighed, L, the fulcrum, F, and the weight, W, are in a straight line. If the length $LF = FW$, and the load and weight are the same, they balance, which is the only accurate weighing we can get—otherwise the heavier goes to the bottom (see dotted line), merely showing which is heavier—not how much. Thus we would need a lot of different weights, or the means of hanging W at varying distances from F, or springs instead of weights.

If however L, F, and W are held at right angles by a bent rod (Fig. 2), the more L weighs than W, the further down L will go to reach equilibrium. The trouble is that the movement down is not proportional to the increase in weight of L. A radial scale, as shown, would have to be graduated with decreasing spaces, becoming less accurate and harder to read. This inequality is shown in Fig. 3: the resultant force of a given load at a given distance from the fulcrum is the product of the downward thrust (here called L) and the *horizontal* distance between the load and the fulcrum is x. Thus, for L to balance W, the equation is $xL = yW$, from which we can see that if L is almost at the bottom, x would be close to zero, and L would have to be enormous to balance yW. *Question:* What fairly simple arrangement of this balance can be made so that an *evenly graduated* scale will show the weight of L, without changing or moving W?

57

HYDRAULIC INFERENCE

Water is poured into an exactly cubical 3½ qt. casserole, near its corner. The water rises to the halfway mark, stops for a while, and then continues to rise at exactly half its previous rate. The reason is that there is an empty pot of inconsiderable thickness inside, attached to the bottom so it doesn't float. What are its most likely proportions and shape?

58

THE STRIPED WHATSIS

The figure shows a version of a merchandising emblem. Describe the form that it indicates, giving number of sides, edges, twists, etc., and making germane comments.

59

THE TERRI TURNOVER

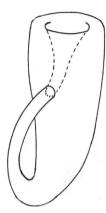

Figure 1 shows a Klein bottle, which has only one side, and a hole through which the neck passes, although this self-intersection is not supposed to exist in the imaginary, ideal version. It is known that a torus—for example, an inner tube—can, if it has a hole in it, be pulled through the hole and in a sense be turned inside out—in a sense, because it is then topologically distorted almost beyond recognition (Fig. 2).

A hollow torus has two sides, but a Moebius strip has only one, and it is meaningless to speak of turning the latter inside out. The question here is whether a model of the Klein bottle can be turned inside out in any meaningful sense, and if so, to what extent must its appearance differ from the way it started?

Question 2

What proportions must a torus have so that when inverted it will have the same proportions as before, if that is possible?

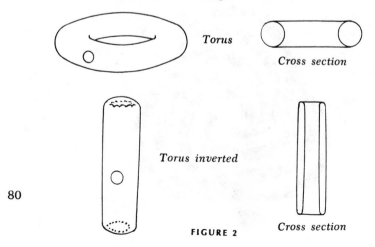

Torus

Cross section

Torus inverted

FIGURE 2

Cross section

60

THE HEAVY CHEST

A chest weighing 200 lb. had been placed against a thin iron pillar, P in the figure, on a tesselated floor, the squares of which measured 1 ft. The chest measured 3 x 4 in. The owner could not lift that much, and he wanted the chest on the other side of P; as shown by the dotted lines, but still facing toward P. The chest could not be slid, but he could lift half its weight fairly easily, and thus turn it, pivoting on one corner. In this way he managed to get it where he wanted it, in a series of continuous, single turns, pivoting on one leg at each turn. He was able to determine the precise positions by the tesselation on the floor. F indicates the front of the chest. The size of the pillar can be ignored. What was the method, and precise number of turns? *Answer on page 82, Figure 1.*

Continued on next page

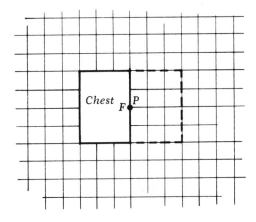

60 Continued

Question 2

He found another chest, also 3 by 5 in., against no obstruction, but near to another thin post (Fig. 2), and he wanted to move it to the position shown by the dotted lines: show how he did it.

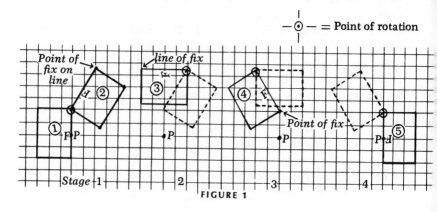

— ⊙ — = Point of rotation

FIGURE 1

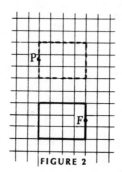

FIGURE 2

61

THE PILE AND THE PATRIOT

At Fort Ticonderoga a soldier was told to make a pile of cannon balls. He began with a square arrangement of the first layer (Fig. 1). The second layer fitted over the spaces, S (hereinafter called squinches), producing an arrangement like the first. When the pyramid was complete, he decided to put a flag at the top, and removed the top ball, but when he tried to put the stick in the squinch where the ball had been he found another ball vertically below, which prevented it from going down far enough to stay upright.

Continued on next page

FIGURE 1

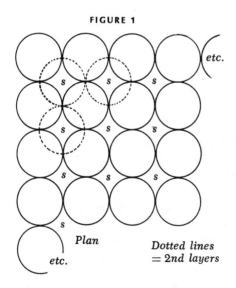

Plan

Dotted lines
= 2nd layers

etc.

FIGURE 2

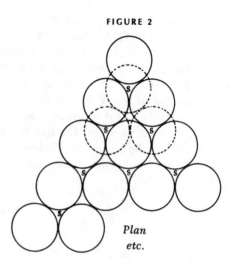

Plan
etc.

Then he began again with a triangular base (Fig. 2). In this case the second layer could not be put in all the squinches because they were too close together, so he chose the ones marked S. It will be noticed that the layers— all of the same triangular arrangement—were horizontally more closely packed than in the first arrangement. When the triangular pyramid was finished he again tried to stick a flag in the top squinch, but failed for the same reason as before. His third attempt succeeded.

In experimenting with marbles we would have to put a frame around the bottom layer to keep them from being pushed aside by the subsequent layers, but since cannon balls are very heavy they make depressions in the ground which prevent rolling. All three arrangements the soldier made are examples of normal (or close) piling. If the second layer in the square (first) arrangement were placed vertically above the first layer it would not be stable, for each ball in the second layer would be balanced on one directly under it, and unless the frame continued upward they would roll off. (This latter arrangement is not considered normal piling.) In solving the problem, the reader is advised not to use actual balls—they get in each other's way and slide all over the place unless one uses moth balls (and aside from smelling dreadful, they aren't accurate spheres).

Question 1

What was the soldier's third and successful method? Also explain how the three methods relate to one another. *Answer on page 203.*

Question 2

In starting with method two (triangular), we eventually produce tilted planes of square-arranged balls, and the same polyhedra as with method one; is it possible to start with method one (square) and get the polyhedra associated with method three, and at some angle produce the continuous holes?* If not, show why, and explain fully, with diagrams.

Continued on next page

Do not turn page: answer to Question 2 begins on next page.

Answer 2

All three arrangements are shown in the plan. In the second and third the polyhedra occur in the plan also, as shown in Figs. 3 and 4 (pages 203–204). The lower △10,11,12 in the last polyhedron is covered by the top △1,2,3. The first arrangement (Fig. 8) gives the polyhedron at an angle of 55° — and is hard to recognize. It is like Fig. 5, but turned to one side like the top of Fig. 6, and tilted toward us so that the square 3,2,6,7 is seen straight on, and coinciding with the square 9,4,10,12. (All the numbers conform to Figs. 5 and 6 on page 205.)

The center balls of the polyhedra have been left out. To see these relationships it is best to make cardboard models. Number the vertexes, but leave the *top* triangles empty, so that one

FIGURE 8

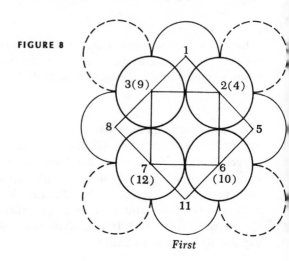

First

can look through to see where vertexes coincide at the different angles of view. In the second polyhedron we show the far edges pale, and the front edges dark. Numbers in brackets are hidden vertexes, i.e., behind the other, non-bracketed numbers. The dotted circles, Fig. 8, are part of the *second layer*, containing 1,5,11,8; 9,4,10,12 are in the bottom layer.

For Answer to last part of Question 2 on page 85, return to page 86.

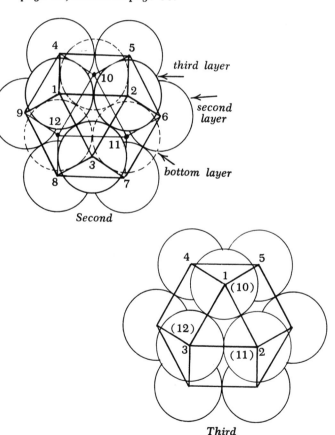

Second

Third

62

THE PILLAR OF CHIOS

The ruler of the ancient Greek island of Chios was explaining to two goldsmiths that he'd come into a little money, and wanted the new monumental pillar changed. It was cylindrical, and he wanted it covered with solid gold, but the gold was to form four equal hemicylindrical projecting moldings, the plan being as shown in the figure. Where these four surfaces met they were to form right angles with one another, and exactly at the surface of the existing pillar.

One of the goldsmiths was rather deaf, and thought what was wanted was a solid square pillar, the four corners of which were to fit exactly in the cylindrical surface of the one it was to replace (see dotted lines in the figure). The goldsmiths were then asked to estimate the amount of gold needed.

To what extent did their estimates differ? We are to assume that both calculations were correct on the basis of what each thought were the requirements.

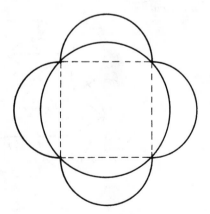

63

LITERARY QUIZ

The title "Father of" so-and-so has been popularly given to many people: their names are given in the second column, and you are to match these with their putative offspring in the first column.

1 Angling	( )	Abraham
2 Church History	( )	Aeschylus
3 Comedy	( )	Aquinas
4 English Cathedral Music	( )	Aristophanes
5 English Poetry	( )	Ascham
6 English Prose	( )	Athanasius
7 Epic Poetry	( )	Boccaccio
8 Fathers	( )	Chaucer
9 Good Works	( )	Eusebius
10 Greek Music	( )	Francis I
11 Greek Tragedy	( )	St. Gregory of Nyssa
12 History	( )	Hippocrates
13 Italian Prose	( )	Homer
14 Jests	( )	Herodotus
15 Letters	( )	Miller (Joe)
16 Lies	( )	Mississippi
17 Medicine	( )	Mohammed II (Turkey)
18 Moral Philosophy	( )	Palestrina
19 Music	( )	Rabelais
20 Orthodoxy	( )	Satan
21 Ridicule	( )	Tallis
22 The Faithful	( )	Terpander
23 Waters	( )	Walton

64

THUNDER ON THE RIGHT

A man at P talks to a friend at F, by phone, and hears a clap of thunder on the phone first, and then ten seconds later from just outside (assume sound goes a mile in 5 sec.).

"Did you hear that?" says the friend. "I think it's coming this way from the sea. I better close the windows, so hold on."

While he is waiting, the first man calculates the locus of the possible positions of S, the source of sound.

Question 1

Describe it, and give proof.

When F comes back to the phone he says, "Incidentally, I counted the seconds between the flash and the sound: it was just 3 mi. away."

Question 2

On hearing the latter, P was able to tell his friend F the exact direction of S from F. What was it?

65

TWO TRIANGLES

We have two identical obtuse-angled triangles, cut out of cardboard. As shown in Fig. 1, they are arranged edge to edge, and in Fig. 2 overlapping, forming different quadrilaterals, the second with a reentrant angle. We want to find how many different quadrilaterals (including the two shown) can be so formed. To be eligible the arrangement must be geometrically determined by point-to-point, edge-to-edge, and point-to-edge contact, and combinations of these. For example, Fig. 3 is not determined, because A can be at varying places on BC, and D at varying places on BE.

Continued on next page

FIGURE 1

FIGURE 2

FIGURE 3

Also Fig. 4 is not determined, since *AB* can slide on *CD*. Figure 5 is a pentagon, though correctly determined.

Either triangle may be inverted, giving its mirror image, as in Fig. 2, but not both triangles, for that would give mirror images of the complete quadrilaterals, which are not allowed. The reader is advised to make accurate reproductions of the given triangles in thin cardboard, since a quite small deviation of the proportions will alter the number of possible arrangements. The answers are in two parts, with the more obvious quadrilaterals given first, and then the total number given; so if the reader has not found the full total, check with the first part first, and then try to find the rest.

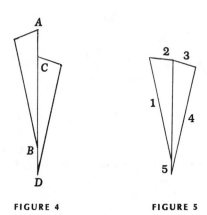

FIGURE 4   FIGURE 5

A SUBMISCELLANY OF SHORT PUZZLES
More or Less from
Everyday Life

These puzzles are slightly inconsequential and do not quite strictly follow the rules of style. They must be read attentively, because the wording is sometimes tricky or overliteral. Some depend on observation, some on previous knowledge, some on rather offbeat reasoning. The reader is warned to watch for the unexpected.

1   *TRANSPARENT OBJECT.* What transparent object becomes less transparent when wiped with a clean cloth? (It is found in many households.)

2   *ICICLES.* Which of these probably saw more icicles more than 2 in. long during her life: Queen Elizabeth I, of England (1533-1603), or an American Indian woman living in upstate New York during the same years?

3   *RODIN'S THINKER.* What is unusual about the pose of Rodin's statue, "The Thinker"?

4   *BLUE DRINK.* How can a bartender who is fresh out of Blue Curaçao mix a bright, sky-blue drink, using only the potables to be found in a well-stocked bar (e.g., food coloring would not)?

5   *VERBALIZED NUMBER.* If you hear someone who is ordering a number of items say: "Send us nine hundred and ninety-nine thousand, nine hundred and ninety-nine million, and one," what would probably be the first thing you would notice about him if you had never heard him before?

6   *CHAIN REACTION.* In giving an example of chain reaction (in everyday life), most popular-scientists describe a floor covered with mousetraps on which are balanced metal balls, so that when one trap is sprung the three or four balls on it fall on other traps, which do likewise, etc. Give a more common example.

7 *COUNT THE OBJECTS*. Without moving your hands, count the things shown below (Fig. 1); a dot inside a square is two things; the letter *A* is one. Give the method used. Time limit, 1½ min.

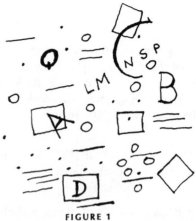

FIGURE 1

8 *BARLEY, MARBLES, ETC.* If you put a half cup of uncooked barley, a dozen (lead) buckshot, three glass marbles, and some cork fragments in a tumbler, and shake or vibrate the lot, what will be their relative arrangement finally? (Figure 2 gives their sizes.)

9 *NORTH AMERICA AND EUROPE.* How close does any part of North America come to being as far east as any part of Europe?

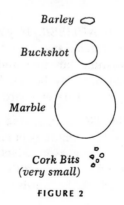

FIGURE 2

96

10 *GREAT CIRCLE.* If all the seas were frozen over, and you were standing at the corner of Fifth Avenue and Forty-second Street in New York City (Fig. 3), which of the four routes would take you nearest, and soonest, to Rome, Italy, provided you walked in a straight path or great circle? ("Soon-est" here means *soonest to the nearest point to Rome.*)

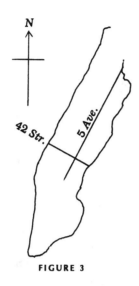

FIGURE 3

11 *NEXT TO NEW YORK.* Which city in the world is the next biggest in population to New York City (as of 1968)?

12 *FLOATING COFFEE.* If you take a small, dry alumi-num pot, put a heaping tablespoonful of dry drip-grind coffee in the middle in a small heap, and carefully pour down the side into the pot a cup of water so that it more than covers the coffee, estimate the fraction of coffee floating on the surface after a few seconds.

13 *TWO-DIGIT NUMBERS.* To be done in the head in half a minute: How many two-digit, positive whole numbers are there?

14 *RAIN ON THE ROOF.* When rain falls straight down on a roof which is tilted at 45° (Fig. 4), there is less rain per unit area than if the roof were level (Fig. 5). This being the case it would seem that rain falling vertically on level ground would give it more of a wetting than the same rain would if it fell at an angle, because of wind. Why is this not so?

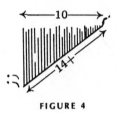

FIGURE 4

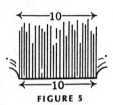

FIGURE 5

15 *BOX AT EDGE.* Sitting on a table, projecting slightly more than half its width over the edge, is a cardboard box (Fig. 6). Owing to something inside it, it remains in this position. When the table is bumped up *vertically* the box falls. Its contents is to be found in most households; what is it?

Then there is an exactly similar box, but projecting *less* than halfway over the edge; in this case it can be made to fall without bumping, touching or imparting any pressure to it or the table, even indirectly. How? What is in it?

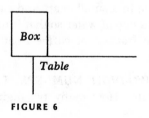

FIGURE 6

16 *LEAKY BALLOON.* A child's rubber balloon was left in the attic resting on a box and an old-fashioned trunk with a hemicylindrical lid, as in the figure. The balloon was so thin that its outline may be considered a circle, but it leaked and sank as it shrank. What is the locus of its center, C, as it lowered until it fell? The edge, E, may be considered as a point.

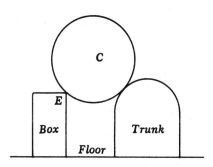

17 *MIDPAGE IN MANUSCRIPT.* From a manuscript, handwritten on both sides of the paper, we remove the middle sheet; its two sides are numbered six and seven. How long is it?

18 *OBLONG STATE.* Most states of the United States are at least partly bounded by arbitrary straight lines—that is to say, they appear so on a Mercator's projection map: Which, if any, are completely rectangular? Which, if any, have no straight lines as boundaries?

19 *WATER FROM PAN.* A saucepan half-full of water is on the floor. Is it possible to get about a teaspoonful of water from it into a cup, without spilling any or putting the cup or anything else below the level of the saucepan's brim, or raising any part of the saucepan?

20 *BOOKSHELF.* You build a single-shelf bookcase for an encyclopedia of twenty-odd volumes. First you measure the dimensions of a volume, 9 by 12 in., and then put them in a pile and measure the total to get the length of the single shelf, about 30 in. Allowing an extra inch in height and depth from front to back, you make the bookcase. What is liable to go wrong?

21   *DOFFING OR DONNING.* Why is it so much easier to take a fairly tight sweater off, if you wear glasses, without them being displaced, than it is to put the sweater on without them being displaced?

22   *GIBRALTAR.* Figure 7 shows a view of the Rock of Gibraltar. In between it and us is an old weather vane with the pointer and letters missing, but here indicated as *A, B, C, D,* with *B* toward us. Which arm points most nearly toward Morocco?

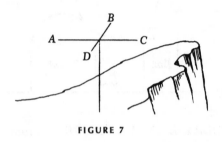

FIGURE 7

23   *BIBLE QUOTE.* To whom did Jesus say, "Get thee behind me . . ."?

24   *BOX FITTING.* A certain very common commodity is sold in boxes, arranged in two rows; the objects are all identical, and if one were removed, we would be able to tell which, in spite of the fact that they are slightly elastic and would fill the gap. What are they?

25   *FOLDING* TIMES. This is a question not of theory, but actual practice: A single sheet of *The New York Times,* opened out flat, measures approximately 22 by 30 in., if folded in half it will be 15 by 22 in. (like one printed page). Will its proportions be as 15 to 22, or 22 to 30 when folded in half a total of ten times?

26   *TILTING DISH.* An oval (quasi-elliptical) china dish is on a table: which point on the rim of the dish requires the least downward pressure to lift the opposite edge? Why? (Or does it make no difference?)

27 *CORN IN BAG.* How many shucked ears of fresh corn can one fit into a thin polyethylene bag, about 8 by 10 in. (the *very* thin kind that some bread comes wrapped in), in 10 sec.?

28 *SAME HEIGHT.* What single physical factor makes it more advantageous to the housewife to have all grocery boxes, bottles, etc., that are not kept in the refrigerator, uniform in height rather than in the other two dimensions?

29 *TORN CARD.* It is impossible in actuality, but assuming that one could tear a playing card in two, put the halves together and tear again (getting four), put them together again and tear, and so on 52 *times,* and piled up the pieces, how high would the stack be? Estimate within 100 percent.

30 *BEAR AND PENGUIN.* A bear walks due south 1 mi., then due east 1 mi., then due north 1 mi. He is a polar bear and he has nothing else to do. He is close to the Arctic Circle. The question is this: The bear is 3 mi. from the sea and can run twice as fast as a penguin, who has just woken, and is also in his natural habitat. He is due south of the bear and 9 mi. from the sea, and can swim twice as fast as the bear. How close can the bear get to the penguin?

31 *REMOVE WATER.* Put a small glass bowl, about 2 in. deep and 3½ in. across, in the sink, run in enough water to come almost a quarter-inch above the rim of the small bowl. Using a teaspoon, is it possible to remove enough water from the bowl by speed and efficiency, so that it floats? The teaspoon may only be put *inside* the bowl; not under it.

32 *CHANGED EQUATION.* A blackboard has an equation on it; to the left of the equal sign is one symbol, and to the right three symbols. A boy remarks that if the symbol to the left of the sign were inverted, and one of the three to the right were erased, the equation would still be true, and contain no redundant or unnecessary symbols. What is the equation? (The line in a fraction counts as a symbol.)

33 *NORTHERNMOST.* Excluding Alaska, what is the most northernly part of the United States?

34   *LETTER CODE*. If we are told that certain letters in the words "Standard Oath" represent something to do with a number series, what should the next letters be?

35   *MEASURING TREE*. There is a pine tree that looks about 100 ft. tall, about 150 ft. away from the house, and slightly downhill. We can get to it by walking around a pond. Our only means of measuring is a 6-ft. tape measure. What is the simplest way to find its height within 10 percent?

36   *HOW MANY KINGS?* Guess within 30 percent how many kings have been crowned in England since the Norman Conquest.

37   *TESSELATION*. In the floor of a Gothic church is the tesselated figure shown here, consisting of three equal arcs in an equilateral triangle, measuring 2 ft. to the side. As simply as possible, give, and prove, the area of the dark part.

38   *QUIZ IN VERSE*.

Oh, what's the past tense of Beware?
Do we say "He Bewore being caught"?
Should we use the same usage with Fare?
And what is the present of Wrought?

Can a wheelwright be said to Wright Wheels?
Should Sluice follow Loose into Sluisen?
And this oral philologist feels
That Mongoose & Son are Mongoosen.

Surely more than one Bus should be Bi;
Might not Might in the past become Mought?
And Trew is the perfect of Try—
But *what* is the present of Wrought?

39 *OPPOSITE STATES.* What two very familiar things, that are alike in a certain important respect, are in opposite states in that respect when described by the same term?

40 *PANAMA CANAL.* If you are at the Atlantic end of the Panama Canal and sail along it to the Pacific end, how many miles west will you have traveled?

41 *DOUSING CIGARETTE.* How can a well-lighted cigarette be put out in less than 30 sec. without using any liquid, or blowing, or touch any part except the unlit half? Nothing is needed except what can be found in most homes.

42 *EASTERNMOST.* What and where is the easternmost point in the United States of America?

43 *ALPHABET SPOKEN.* In saying the alphabet the words we utter have in some cases initial letters that differ from the letter we refer to; for example, we say "ex" and "em." In how many cases does this occur?

44 *RHYME PUZZLE.*
I'll give R-α dog, oh ϕ!
All he liked was cherry π.
The cat will η fish and μ.
$_0$-ology!

(Question: What does the last line mean?)

45 *SOUTHERNMOST.* Name the southernmost points of Europe, Africa, and South America.

46 *WHEELS.* What vehicle has an odd number (greater than three) of supporting wheels? (For example, steering or transmission wheels wouldn't count. And airplanes and boats are not allowed.)

47 *WET SPOON.* When the professor started spooning sugar into his coffee, Mrs. M. said, "The spoon's wet—it won't let go of all the sugar."

"I know," he said, "but I stir with it, also."

"Then you get more than you bargained for, because it sticks to the bottom of the spoon, also. That is, unless you want a little more than a spoonful."

"No; I like an exact measurement, but with the number I take, it comes out just right." How many did he take?

48 *PINCH-PENNY*. A man was sending a lot of letters by airmail. He had an accurate scale for weighing, but he always took the letters to be weighed at the post office. Why?

49 *TWO LIQUIDS*. What two liquids, which are to be found in most average homes, when poured into the same clean empty container, neither mix, flavor, nor contaminate each other, and can be quickly and easily separated (no heating allowed)?

50 *LONGEST SENTENCE*. What is the longest sentence in two words in English?

ANSWERS TO PUZZLES

ROLLERS

Neither.

Since the top surface of the lower ball is in non-skidding contact with the bottom surface of the top ball, we can imagine a sheet of paper, *s*, between them, moving to the left. When *s* moves *x* inches, the center, *a*, of the bottom ball moves ½*x* inches in the same direction. The same is true of the center, *b*, of the top ball; thus *b* remains vertically above *a*, regardless of the direction of motion.

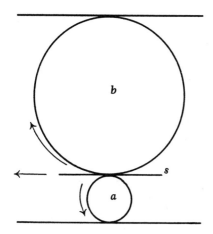

2

OWL'S EGGS

The crank.

The formula for the volume of a cylinder is $\pi r^2 h$, where r is the radius, and h is the height. If we call the radius of the pot 1, then its volume up to the water level is πh. Since h is the diameter of the egg, we call the egg's radius r, and the cylinder's volume becomes $2\pi r$. The formula for the volume of a sphere is $(4/3)\pi r^3$. Thus the volume of water, V, is $2\pi r - 4/3\pi r^3$. To find the value of r that gives the greatest value, i.e., the most water, we would have to use calculus; but the question was which of the two men got the nearest answer. We divide both sides of the equation by 2π: $\dfrac{V}{2\pi} = r - \dfrac{2}{3}r^3$.

From this we see that to get the value for r that gives the maximum value for V, we can disregard the 2π. Therefore the answer is independent of π, and the man with the more accurate ruler got the nearest answer, since he had the right measurement for the pot.

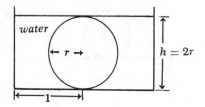

CONICAL HELIX

A semicircle with radius $= 1$, drawn on the flattened surface of the cone, and with PA as diameter.

Since the base of the cone has a diameter of 1 and $PA = 2 =$ the cone's (tilted) radius, the perimeter of the base $= \pi =$ one-fourth the perimeter of a circle with a radius of 2. Therefore the flattened segment is a fourth of a circle.

In Fig. 1, P'' is the repeat of P, and C is the center of semicircle, PIA. Semicircle PIA fills the requirements, because it is tangent to the quarter-circle, $PP'P''$, at P, it is tangent to radius $P''A$ at A, and it intersects, at I, the radius $P'A$, the bisector of $\angle P''AP$ at $45°$, since IC is perpendicular to PA.

To make a model, it is best to put the semicircle—the helix-to-be—on PA, extending outward (Fig. 2), and cut the whole figure from one piece of paper. Then when rolled into a cone, with the semicircle on the outside, the latter gives the helix with its edge.

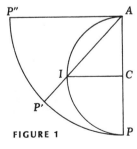

FIGURE 1

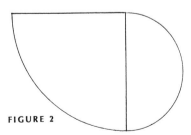

FIGURE 2

Answer 2

The ratio of the flat model's greatest dimension to its least dimension equals ϕ.

$P''Q$ is greatest if the line passes through C, the center of semicircle AQP, and AP, its least.

$$\phi = \frac{\sqrt{5}+1}{2}$$

$$x^2 = 2^2 + 1, \text{ so } x = \sqrt{5}$$

$$P''Q = \sqrt{5} + 1, \quad AP = 2$$

$$\frac{P''Q}{AP} = \frac{\sqrt{5}+1}{2} = \phi$$

Q.E.D.

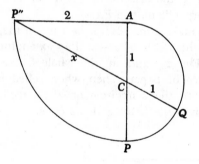

THE OWL ISLAND FLAG

$h = 2$ ft.

In the figure, the vertical lines, ll, represent the available space with width $= 4$ ft. The red square, R, is put at one side. Since R is always square, the 45° diagonal is the locus of its free corner, and the rectangle to its right, with height h, and width w, is the total area of white left. Change scale, making $W = 2$:

When $h = w = 1$, then the area of white equals 1. If h and w are unequal by the amount $2n$, area $= (1 + n) \times (1 - n) = 1 - n^2$, which is less than 1; therefore maximum area is got when h is 2 ft., in original scale.

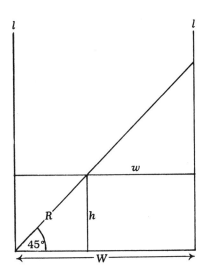

5

PSEUDO-MOEBIUS STRIP

A flat, hollow square (two sides, two edges, zero twists). The four corners made at the intersection of the dotted lines give the four corners of the square. When loop B is cut along the dotted line (see page 23), loop A, whether cut along the dotted line or not, can be opened out and untwisted, regardless of the number of its twists. But it probably needs clairvoyance to visualize it.

Answer 2

In no way. Regardless of how far y were moved, the length of each resulting edge would be unaltered, and the way everything is connected would be the same as before.

THE BUTLER AND THE CRUMBS

"*Now* look! You missed some in the middle!"

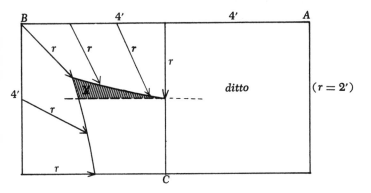

Area X, half of which is shown, was beyond his reach. He could not reach the center line, dotted, because when walking along the top side, *AB*, he pushed "directly toward *C*" (see arrows), a constant distance, *r*, instead of pushing at right angles from *AB*, as he should have done. So the maid had to clean up X.

7

THE THREE CLOCKS

I find an alarm clock, and I can see that it was set back because the alarm indicator is at six, and we always have it set to go off at seven. It is in the fall.

8

SLIT STRIPS

Two loops, unlinked, one with a right-hand twist, the other with a left-hand twist.

The reason is that there are two ways of making the nonself-intersecting loop, with right-hand or left-hand twists (R and L, Fig. 1 each of them remains the same when turned top to bottom or back to front). To analyze them we examine the edges.

When we cut either of them down the center, the resultant halves conform to the two edges (Fig. 2) which can be seen to cross the same way and to be linked, at X. When the strip goes through a slit we get a new arrangement (Fig. 3), in which edge *A* goes to the right of itself, and *B* to the left of itself. Thus the two halves will have opposite twists, and can be seen not to link together. This form is symmetrical.

Continued on next page

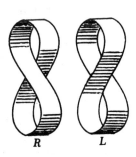

FIGURE 1

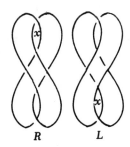

FIGURE 2

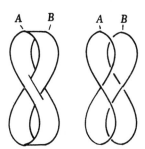

FIGURE 3

115

8 Continued

Answer 2

A will have four half-twists and no knot; B will have eight half-twists and a knot. Again we examine the edges. Figure 1 shows the uncut form of A, and its edge (both A and B are single-edged), isolated and then further simplified. We see that A is in the form of a Moebius strip, and when cut lengthwise, gives the same result, an unknotted single loop with four half-twists.

Figure 2 shows the isolated edge of B, which has the form of a three-half-twist Moebius strip, and when further simplified, is in the form of a trefoil knot. The point is that A and B are not true mirror images of one another; Fig. 3 shows the mirror image of A.

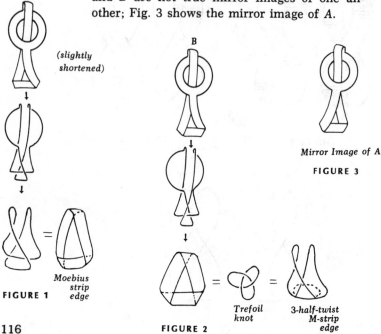

A

(slightly shortened)

B

Mirror Image of A

FIGURE 3

Moebius strip edge

FIGURE 1

Trefoil knot

3-half-twist M-strip edge

FIGURE 2

116

(For further discussion of twists, etc., see page 94, *Experiments in Topology*, Barr, T. Y. Crowell.)

THE POT ON THE CROSSPIECES

21¼ in.

In the plan, I is the intersection of the cross-pieces; AI, BI, and CI are respectively the 6-, 8-, and 15-in. lengths of the crosspieces cut off by the pot, and AD is the diameter of the pot.

$$AB = \sqrt{6^2 + 8^2} = 10$$
$$AC = \sqrt{8^2 + 15^2} = 17$$

Since $\angle ABD$ is subtended by a diameter and B is on the circle, it is a right angle. $\angle \alpha = \angle \alpha'$, because both are subtended by AB. Finally, $\angle AIC$ is a right angle. Hence, $\triangle ABD$ is similar to $\triangle AIC$.

$$\frac{AD}{AB} = \frac{AC}{AI} \therefore AD = \frac{10 \times 17}{8} = 21.25 \text{ or } 21\tfrac{1}{4}$$

Continued on next page

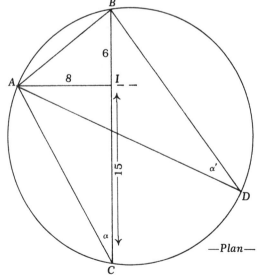

—*Plan*—

Answer 2

The unseen intersection is also exactly on a mark: 6 in.

Proof: Since they are both subtended by the chord AC, $\angle \alpha = \angle \alpha'$

$\therefore$ rt. $\triangle ABI$ is similar to rt. $\triangle CID$

$$\therefore \frac{x}{CI} = \frac{BI}{AI}$$

$$\therefore \quad x = \frac{2 \times 3}{1}$$

$$= 6$$

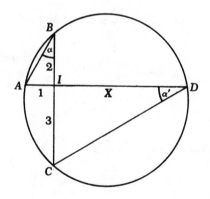

FOR SCRABBLE PLAYERS

Answer is deferred (see next page). In case the
reader has not yet solved the puzzle, here is the
situation—or a possible one—before the play
that will give the required score; and the seven
letters he holds, from which the word is to be
made: G, I, L, Q, T, Y and Z.

COCOS is the preferred spelling.

AR is a variant of ARE, a metric system
measure.

DOR is a beetle (not to be confused with
Paul, or Ringo, etc.).

MEL is Latin for *honey* to English speaking
pharmacists, but given in dictionaries
without the bars, ||.

Continued on next page

```
D       B E R A [T] E D
I             V         A
S             O         S
J             C O C O S
O       P I K E     H   A R         W
I D O L   U T     I   G A M M A
N O V A   D       L   A I   E X
  R A N   U       I   I N   L
```

Only the lower half of the board is needed.
□ is center square.

10

Answer

TRANQUILIZINGLY (scores 1148).

As can be seen, the word covers three triple-word-score squares, and $3 \times 3 \times 3 = 27$, so the scoring is

TRANQUILIZ-			
INGLY	gives	999	(27×37)
DISJOINT	"	48	(3×16)
WAXY	"	51	(3×17)
Premium for us-			
ing all 7 letters	"	50	
	Total	1148	

```
D        B E R  A T E D
I                V       A
S                O       S
J               C O C O S
O        P I K E    H   A R            W
I  D O L    U T    I    G A M M A
N O V A    D      L    A I    E X
T R A N Q U  I  L  I  Z  I N G L Y
```

AREA OF ROOF

200 sq. ft.

Since the profile we see of the roof is an equilateral triangle, the altitude, a, of each triangular face must be equal to the width of the shed,
10 ft. (Fig. 1). This is twice the altitude of
each of the four triangles that would make up
the 10×10 ft. plan of the shed (Fig. 2). The
figures need not be drawn, because they can
easily be visualized. (When the altitude of a
figure is doubled, the area is doubled.)

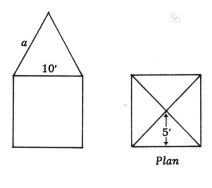

Plan

FIGURE 1   **FIGURE 2**

12

PAPER-FOLDING

Two folds, altogether.

In each case opposite corners are brought together and creased. In the figures we have multiplied the dimensions; in the short rectangle by four and in the longer one by three. With the first the dimensions of the right triangles become 4, 5, and 3, and with the second they become 3, 5, and 4. Thus they are similar, and the corresponding angles α and α' are equal (also β and β'). (Proof of the relationships as in Puzzle 43.)

Proof for short paper:

with width $= 1$, length $= 2$,

we change the scale as shown in the figure (Proof for this one is similar)

$a + b = 2$, $\therefore b = 2 - a$; $c = 1$

by Pythagoras,

$a^2 = 1 + b^2 = 1 + 4 - 4a + a^2$

$\therefore 4a = 1 + 4 + a^2 - a^2$,

thus in the original scale:

$a = 5$, $c = 4$, and $b = 3$

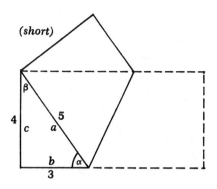

(short)

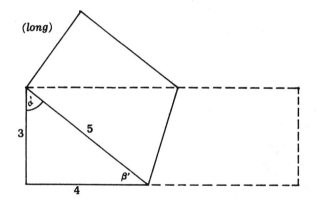

(long)

13

THE TWO PYRAMIDS

A cube, with height $= \frac{1}{2} \sqrt{2}$, with length of pyramids' edge $= 1$. If a square has sides equaling $\frac{1}{2} \sqrt{2}$, its diagonal equals 1 (Fig. 1).

Figure 2 shows a cube with edge equaling $\frac{1}{2} \sqrt{2}$; *ABCD* is the biggest tetrahedron that can be cut from it, leaving four equal three-sided (plus base) pyramids with their apexes at *E*, *F*, *G*, and *H*. They have equilateral triangles for their inner faces—their bases—and the three angles meeting at each apex are right angles. They can be fitted together with their apexes meeting at a point on the ground, as in Fig. 3. Their equilateral faces now form the four sides of the square pyramid. The interior tetrahedron forms, or is, the triangular pyramid. All edges equal 1.

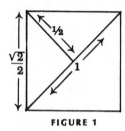

FIGURE 1

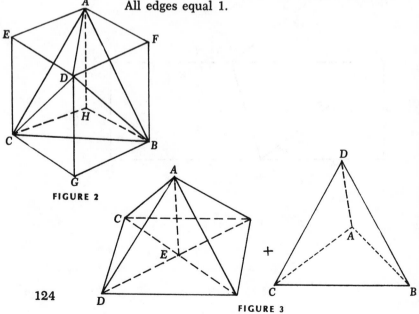

FIGURE 2

FIGURE 3

THE MAN WHO GAVE UP SMOKING

The important clue is the word *rearrange*. By putting the seven-space row in the middle, there is only room for nineteen cigarettes, and four can be removed, as in the figure.

Continued on next page

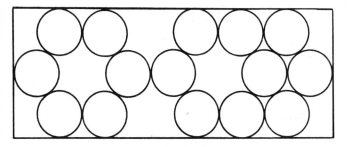

14 ^{Continued}

Answer 2

As shown in the figure. He should not have been surprised at the square being larger, since it holds more circles.

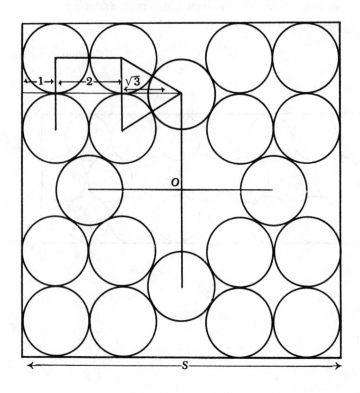

20 circles

$$S = 2(3+\sqrt{3})r$$
$$(= 9.464 \pm appr.)$$
$$(S^2 = 89.5673\pm)$$
4.478 *per.*

Answer 3

As in the figure. The dimensions are self-explanatory.

Continued on next page

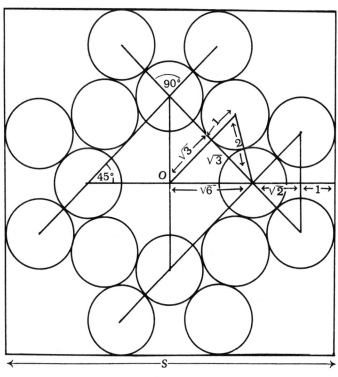

16 circles

$$S = 2(\sqrt{6} + \sqrt{2} + 1)r$$
$$(= 9.72 + appr.)$$
$$S^2 = 94.48 \; appr.$$
$$5.28 \; per.$$

14

Answer 4

The nonrigidity involves the principle of group rotation, which we saw in Fig. 2 in the questions. In Fig. 1, here, no single circle can move alone, but all three can rotate as a group, whereas in Fig. 2 they cannot. It is more clearly shown in Fig. 3, where the circles, dotted, are ignored and we consider their centers. The possible motion of the center of a circle held against a straight line, is another straight line parallel with the first, so here we draw a new triangle (solid), inside the original one (dotted). It is understood that the circles do not have to roll, but can slide against other surfaces.

Another factor of importance in this case is symmetry. Figure 4 shows the bottom half of the arrangement under consideration; if the group *ABC* can rotate when *A* moves along the line *OAH*, its mirror image *ADE*, symmetrical with it about *OAH*, can rotate in the opposite direction, and *A*, which is common to both groups, will move along *OAH*. Similarly with *BFG*, the other mirror image of *ABC*, in which case *B* will move along their line of symmetry,

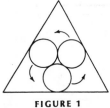

FIGURE 1

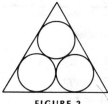

FIGURE 2

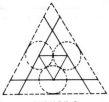

FIGURE 3

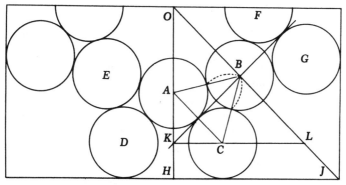

FIGURE 4

OBJ. As in Fig. 3, we draw the triangle *ABC* and decide whether it is free to rotate either or both ways in the triangle *OKL* (with *KL* parallel to *HJ*).

The locus of *B* when *A* moves on *OK*, and *C* on *KL* is known to be an ellipse with its major axis on *BK* (and part of it shown dotted) which is the bisector of the 90° angle, *OKL*, therefore the rotation is possible both ways. Obviously this line of reasoning applies to all the three-groups of circles because of symmetry. It can be seen that there are two possible ways for the distortion of the arrangement to happen; *A* and its three counterparts moving toward *O*, or away from it. If any one of the sixteen circles is fixed, the whole will be rigid; but as Mrs. C. C. realized, none of them is.

Continued on next page

Answer 5

There are two fairly obvious ways; the first (Fig. 1) is to distort a three-row hexagonal arrangement by reducing the vertical space. The second (Fig. 2) starts with a symmetrical hollow hexagon, distorted the same way, but with the square only slightly larger. Both are obviously rigid. The radius of the circles equals 1.

We begin by assuming the drawing of Fig. 1 is correct, in which case the four outer circles have their centers on a square, and by symmetry all the triangles formed by any three contiguous circles will be congruent. Thus the spacing of the centers will divide the square vertically in two, and horizontally in three. For the construction we draw circle A first, and a vertical line AB equal to any three convenient units (here we use two), then at right angles

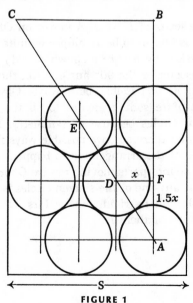

FIGURE 1

to the left draw $BC = $ two units (or four). Join AC; by similar triangles, AC will pass through the centers of circles D and E, and these are found by marking off diameters from A along AC. The rest is easy.

To calculate the size of S: Let $DF = x$; then by proportion $AF = 1.5x$, and by Pythagoras, $x^2 + (1.5x)^2 = 4$; $x = \sqrt{1.2}$ (1.0954...), $S = 2 + 3x$, or 5.286. ... To construct Fig. 2: draw circle with A as center; draw a horizontal through A cutting circle at B; draw a line BB' at 45° to AB, and an arc with radius 2, and center B, to cut BB' at C; draw circle (radius 1) with center C. The rest is easy. To calculate S: draw line $e \perp BC$, line $f \parallel AB$, and line x at right angles to AB. Since $\angle BCC' = 45°$, $x' = x$. $AB = 1$; $e = \sqrt{2}/2$. $AC = 2$; $d^2 = 4 - (2/4)$; $\therefore d = \sqrt{3.5}$; $2x^2 = 3.5$; $x = \sqrt{1.75}$. Since $f = 1/2$, $S = 3 + 2\sqrt{1.75} = 3 + \sqrt{7}$, or 5.64575. ...

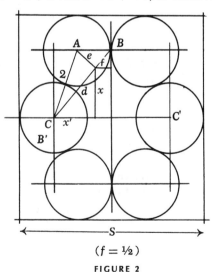

$(f = \frac{1}{2})$

FIGURE 2

15

TETRAHEDRON ANGLES

The third (isolated) right angle (3 in Fig. 1) must be between the two edges, a and c, that meet at the other end of the edge b, which is between the neighboring pair of right angles 1 and 2. Figure 2 shows the same tetrahedron opened out flat like a cardboard model.

Proof: There are 12 facial angles on a tetrahedron, but of the 9, other than the given ones, 1, 2, and 3, we can rule out those marked 0 (Fig. 2), for they are in the right triangles containing paired right angles 1 and 2. Also 0′, since it is at the same apex as 1 and 2. This leaves 4, 5, 6, and 7. We take them in turn: If $4 = 90°$ (Fig. 3):

$$y^2 + z^2 = x^2$$
$$x^2 + b^2 = a^2$$
$$\therefore y^2 + z^2 + b^2 = a^2$$
$$z^2 + b^2 = c^2$$
$$\therefore y^2 + c^2 = a^2$$

and $\angle 7$ is a right angle. The converse of the above shows that if 7 is made a rt. $\angle$, 4 will be one too. If $5 = 90°$ (Fig. 4):

$$x^2 + y^2 = z^2$$
$$b^2 + x^2 = a^2$$
$$b^2 + z^2 = c^2$$
$$\therefore b^2 + x^2 + y^2 = c^2$$
$$\therefore a^2 + y^2 = c^2,$$

and $6 = 90°$. The converse shows that if 6 is made a rt. $\angle$, 5 will be one too.

Q.E.D.

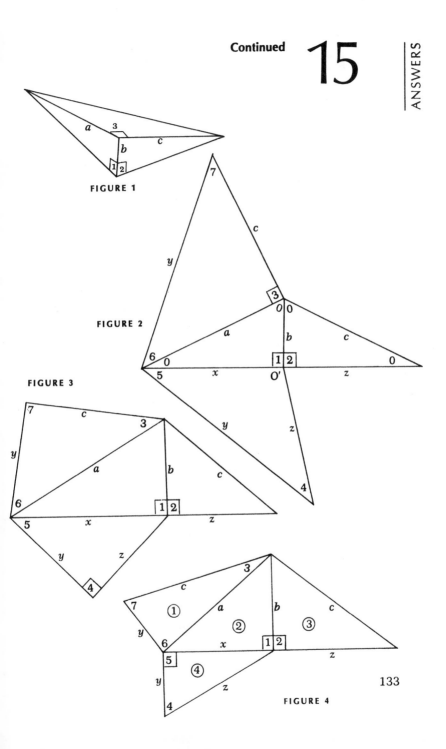

FIGURE 1

FIGURE 2

FIGURE 3

133

FIGURE 4

16

HYPOCYCLOIDS

The curves are identical, but the one in Fig. 2 would be generated in a counterclockwise direction.

It is not necessary to know the equations to these hypocycloids to see that as A' rolls to the left (clockwise around the inside of circle B'), P' starts by moving to the left. Since the circumference of A' is five-sixths that of B', P' will touch B' at a point P'', five-sixths of the lefthand semicircle from T to T', whereupon the same movement will be repeated, counterclockwise.

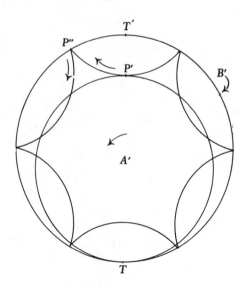

SQUARES ON A CIRCLE

(nonalgebraic):

Eight squares. (With six squares, $r = \dfrac{(\sqrt{2} \times \cot 30°) - \sqrt{2}}{2}$ an irrational number; seven squares is worse.)

By symmetry the diagonals of alternate squares AB, DE, etc., lie on extended radii, AC, DC, etc., which are at right angles. Thus the spaces left between the squares have parallel sides, e.g., $FH \parallel JK$, and we can slide four squares as shown by the arrows until corners such as F and G meet at inner corners of unmoved squares, such as H. By symmetry, the four moved squares will meet at C (see dotted lines).

Therefore r, in this case BC, is the distance moved by F (or G), to H, which is the side of a square, FH, or 1.

Q.E.D.

For the Suspicious:

By symmetry $YC \perp ZC$, $XY = ZC$, and $XZ = YC$

$$XY = 1 + \sqrt{2}/2$$
$$ZC = r + \sqrt{2}/2$$
$$\therefore r = 1$$

Q.E.D.

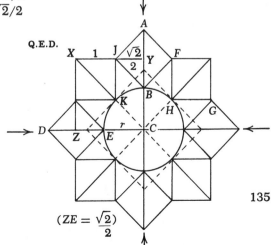

$$\left(ZE = \frac{\sqrt{2}}{2}\right)$$

135

18

THREE COINS

1, 2, and 3—diameters or radii.

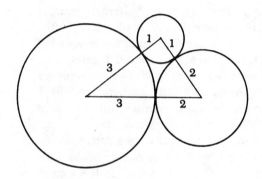

TWO COINS

3 oz. (troy).

When the small coin reaches the point where it tips, its diameter AD must be a chord of the circular hole. A point on the coin's edge that touches the center of the hole, C, will be on CB, with B the center of the coin, and $CB \perp AD$, because $AC = DC$, radii of the hole. Since they are also radii of the coin, $AB = CB$; call this length 1. Then $AC = \sqrt{2}$, and since the coins have the same thickness, their weights are proportional to their areas, which in turn are proportional to the squares of their respective radii. Hence the big coin weighs twice as much as the small one ($\sqrt{2}^2 = 2$).

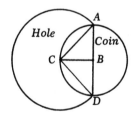

20

THE COIN COLLECTOR'S NIGHTMARE

This construction is best described as very sensitive; the slightest inaccuracy has an exaggerated effect on the result. It is the opposite of those constructions which give very close approximations to unattainable quantities like π, but are mathematically false. The description of the construction is given here, and the proof later, as a second question. Assume the two coins and right-angle corner of the box are drawn, with V as vertex. We omit obvious con-

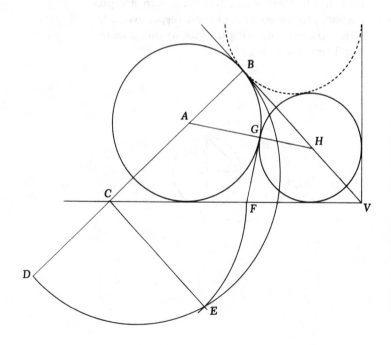

struction details, like bisection, etc. Because of symmetry, as required, we consider only one coin, center A, the other being indicated by a dotted line. Both are tangent at B to a line at 45° through V. Obviously the required circle will have its center on VB.

Draw radius BA and extend to D, intersecting VC at C, and $CD = CA$;

Draw a semicircle with BD as diameter.

Draw CE perpendicular to BD, cutting semicircle at E.

With C as center, mark F on VC (with $CF = CE$).

Draw FG tangent to circle A at G.

Draw AG extended to cut VB at H.

H is the center of the required circle.

Prove the above construction.

Proof: The diagram on the following page is to be regarded as illustrating the following proof, not the previous construction. In it we shall use similar labeling, and add certain necessary lines and points. We start by assuming that the required circle is drawn; we know that it can exist touching both axes through V, and both large circles (the big coins). By symmetry, its center H will be on VB, the bisector of the corner of the box, V. AH joins the centers of the chosen large circle and the required circle, and G is their point of contact. Draw GF perpendicular to AH, with F on CV. Then:

Continued on next page

20 ^{Continued}

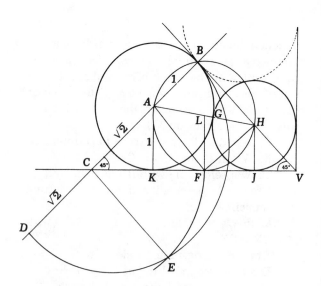

FG is the common tangent of circles A and H.

AB is the radius of circle A, $AB = 1$.

VB is tangent to circle A at B, $\therefore$ $\angle CBV = 90°$, and $\angle BCV = 45°$.

Draw HJ and AK perpendicular to VC; draw FH and FA, and FL with L at midpoint of AH.

FK and FG are tangent to circle A, and FG and FJ to circle H.

$\therefore FK = FG = FJ$; FA bisects $\angle GFK$, and FH bisects $\angle GFJ$.

$\therefore$ $\angle AFH$ is the sum of the halves of the supplementary $\angle$s GFK and GFJ.

$\therefore$ $\angle AFH = 90°$, and since $\angle ABH = 90°$, the points A, B, H, and F are cocyclic, with L as center and ALGH a diameter.

∴ the circle (with center L) through A, B, H, and F can be drawn.

AK is parallel to HJ, $LA = LH$, and $FK = FJ$.

∴ LF is perpendicular to KJ.

∴ CF is tangent to circle L.

By a well-known proposition, the secant $CB : CF = CF : CA$.

∴ $CB/CF = CF/CA$, and obviously $CA = \sqrt{2}$

∴ $\dfrac{1 + \sqrt{2}}{CF} = \dfrac{CF}{\sqrt{2}}$

∴ $CF^2 = \sqrt{2} + 2$.

We now add that part of the original construction which gave the position of F, and from it prove that the value of CF in that construction is equal to the value just given. By another well-known proposition, since DEB is a semicircle on diameter DB,

$CE^2 = CD \times CB$

∴ $CE^2 + \sqrt{2}(\sqrt{2} - 1) = 2 + \sqrt{2}$

∴ $CF^2 = \sqrt{2} + 2$

Q.E.D.

21

THE HI-Φ SET

The diagonal DD' compared to the width of two coins is ϕ. DD' is the greatest dimension of the group, and the line DD' runs through centers B and C.

If we consider the figure at half-scale, so that $AB = 1$, then $AC = 2$, and the hypotenuse $BC = \sqrt{5}$.

BD and CD' are radii, so that $DD' = \sqrt{5} + 1$.

Thus at the original scale, with width $= 1$,
$DD' = \dfrac{\sqrt{5} + 1}{2} = \phi$ (coins x and y are redundant).

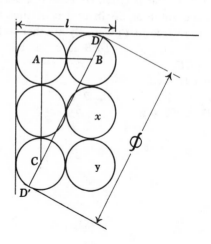

CRYPTARITHMETIC

The clue is the wording; it's in Roman numerals:

$$
\begin{array}{r}
\text{D C V I} \\
\text{− L X V} \\
\hline
\text{D X L I}
\end{array}
\left(\text{or, in Arabic numerals: }
\begin{array}{r}
6\ 0\ 6 \\
-\ 6\ 5 \\
\hline
5\ 4\ 1
\end{array}
\right)
$$

23

ORIGAMETRY

Make the horizontal fold from *A* (Fig. 1); then fold and crease on *AB*, and finally on the full diagonal from *C*.

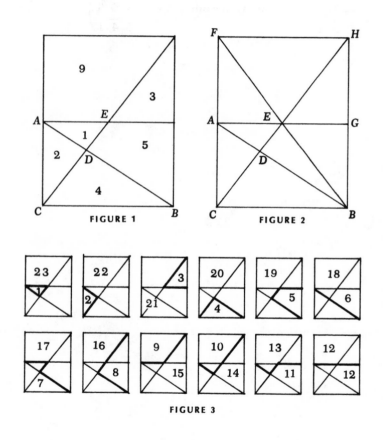

FIGURE 1

FIGURE 2

FIGURE 3

The numerals represent the number of twenty-fourths of each area shown.

To prove, draw the other diagonal FB (Fig. 2). E is the midpoint of FB, and A the midpoint of FC; thus D, the intersection of CE and AB, is the centroid of $\triangle FBC$. Therefore $BD = 2\ AD$, and $CD = 2\ DE$. Triangles AED and ADC have the same altitude. Let the area of AED be 1; then the area of $ADC = 2$. Since the rectangle $AGBC$ is made up of four triangles like AEC, its area $= 12$, and the area of the whole piece of paper $FHBC = 24$. Since $BD = 2\ AD$, the area of $DBC = 4$, and by subtraction the area of quadrilateral $EGBD = 5$. Similarly the area of $HGE = 3$, and $FHEA = 9$. (All these are marked in Fig. 1.)

From this it is easy to see how the twelve patterns shown in Fig. 3 can be made by selecting parts of the given creases, so as to get the twenty-four required fractions.

24

THE HAUBERK

As in the Figure. Rings 1, 2, and 3 form the arrangement shown in Fig. 2 in the question; also 2, 3, and 4; and 3, 4, and 5; etc.

The lord was delighted, but his alchemist was a great believer in even numbers, and particularly admired squares, and said, "It's all very well, but the pattern isn't square, like the ones we make. You've got the rings arranged so that each one has 6 around it. Bet you can't make a square one."

But the armorer did; that is, the rings were arranged in straight lines crossing at right angles—forming squares instead of hexagons. What was the pattern?

Answer 2

As in Fig. 1. There is another arrangement (Fig. 2) which as shown is apparently square, but when pulled in the direction of the arrows becomes Fig. 3, which is the same as the answer to the first question. Fig. 1, here, cannot be thus distorted.

* When X and Y are pulled, rings 1, 2, 4, 5, 10, and 9 form a hexagon around 3, corresponding to the same numbered rings in the answer to the first question, shown here in Fig. 3. Y and X have no counterparts because the pattern was not carried that far.

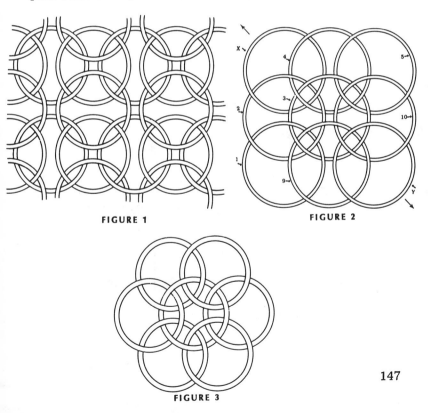

FIGURE 1

FIGURE 2

FIGURE 3

25

MORE ORIGAMETRY

(1) Fold *A* to *B* and make center crease. (2) Fold *A* up to center crease. (3) Fold top edge down at back, level with *A*, making crease *CD* horizontal by aligning first center crease with itself; then bring *A* back to old position (*A*). (4) Fold *AD* to coincide with *CD*, making new crease *DE*. (5) Fold *CB* back making new crease *EF* along *AE*. Flatten out; square *AEGD* is the required one. Let *AB* = 2, then area of paper = 4. In Fig. 3, *AC* = 1 and *AB* = 2; ∴ *CB* = √3. In Fig. 6, area of the square *AEGD* = √3 × √3, which is three-fourths of 4.

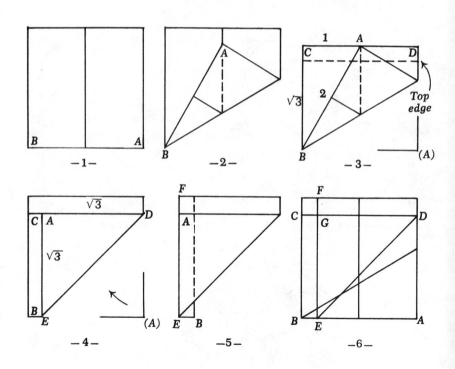

UNIQUE PARTS OF LETTERS

Only one: the top half of S.
It could be got from 8, but we are confined to
the alphabet.

Letters in the top line are made from indicated
parts of letters (heavy) under them.

27

FOR Φ FANS

$x = 2$.

The following equations may be known to the reader, but they can all be easily derived from $\dfrac{a}{a+b} = \dfrac{b}{a}$:

$$\phi^2 = \phi + 1$$

$$\frac{1}{\phi} = \phi - 1, \text{ from which } \phi^2 - \frac{1}{\phi} = 2$$

So, in the original equation in the question, the index of the first expression, $\phi^x - \dfrac{x-1}{\phi} = \phi^2 - \dfrac{2-1}{\phi} = 2$, and the whole equation becomes

$$\phi^2 - \frac{1}{\phi} = 2$$

THE TRUCK GARDENS

The right number of square gardens will fit
into a square whose side is the frontage of the
line of apartment houses, because

$$1^3 + 2^3 + 3^3 + \ldots n^3 = \left(\frac{n(n+1)}{2}\right)^2$$
$$= (1 + 2 + 3 + \ldots n)^2$$

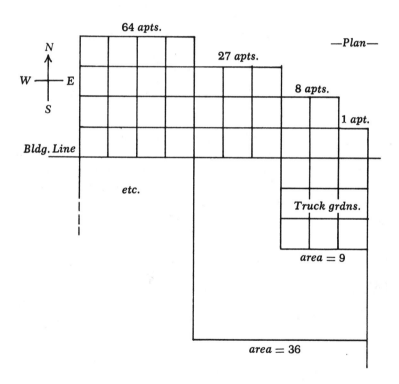

—Plan—

64 *apts.*

27 *apts.*

8 *apts.*

1 *apt.*

N

W —|— E

S

Bldg. Line

etc.

Truck grdns.

area = 9

area = 36

29

Φ ORIGAMETRY

Dotted lines show positions before folding.
Figure 1: fold on diagonal, CB. Figure 2: fold
corner A down to bring AB onto diagonal CB.
$DB : CA = \phi : 1$.

First a ϕ-relationship proof: $\phi = \dfrac{\sqrt{5}+1}{2}$;
$\phi - 1 = \dfrac{1}{\phi}$; and $\sqrt{5} - 1 = 2\phi - 2$ (these can
all be derived from the definition of ϕ).

In Fig. 2, $CB = \sqrt{5}$, and $CA = \sqrt{5} - 1 = 2\phi - 2$. If we make $CA = 1$, then $1 : CA = DB : 2$ and $\dfrac{1}{2\phi - 2} = \dfrac{DB}{2}$

$DB = \dfrac{2}{2\phi - 2} = \dfrac{1}{\phi - 1}$ and since $\phi - 1 = \dfrac{1}{\phi}$

$DB = \phi$

Figure 3 shows that our folded rectangle
can be fitted to the well-known Euclidean construction in which CF is divided by G, so that
$CF : CG = CG : GF$, $(CG = CA)$, in other words,
the ϕ relationship.

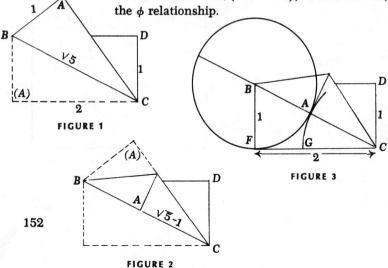

FIGURE 1

FIGURE 2

FIGURE 3

THE COCKEYED KITE

The kitemaker rightly ignored the isosceles triangle as such, and used the formula that says, in any quadrilateral whose diagonals (in this case, the ribs) are at right angles, the sum of the squares of two opposite sides is equal to the sum of the squares of the other two sides:
$20^2 + 9^2 = 15^2 + AD^2$, thus $AD = \sqrt{256} = 16$.

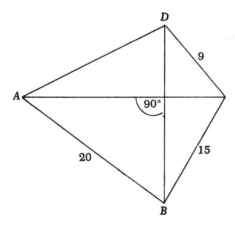

31

MORE Φ ORIGAMETRY

Let side of square equal 2: Figure 1: crease one establishes center of an edge; crease two is a diagonal of a 1×2 rectangle. Figure 2: fold down corner A to make AC lie on crease two, and making BC crease three. Figure 3: fold A back, and make BD, crease four, parallel with AC, by folding so that ED lies on DC. Then $AC/AB = \phi$.

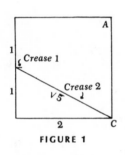

FIGURE 1

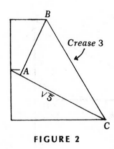

FIGURE 2

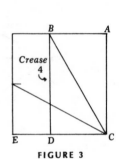

FIGURE 3

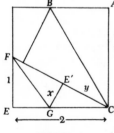

FIGURE 4

Proof:

Figure 4: fold corner E up, so that FE lies on FC. As established in Puzzle 29, $2/y = \phi$, so $y = 2/\phi$. Since $\triangle E'CG$ is similar to $\triangle FCE$,

$$y = 2x$$

$$\therefore 2x = 2/\phi$$

$$\therefore x = 1/\phi, \text{ and } 1/x = \phi$$

FG is the bisector of $\angle EFE'$, $\angle ACF = \angle EFE'$ and BC is the bisector of $\angle ACF$

$$\therefore \triangle ACB \text{ is similar to } \triangle FEG$$

$$\therefore AC/AB = \phi$$

THE BOOKMARK

$\phi - 1$ (or .618...).

The method of folding to get the maximum projection is as follows, shown first with a book of usual proportions:

Since no point on the page can be pulled horizontally farther from the hinge, the motion must be up or down. The diagonal BC (Fig. 1) is the greatest dimension and allows the maximum projection of the corner B when BC rotates upward with C as center. First A is folded up, creasing the page along BC, and flattened again. Turn page to the right (Fig. 2); then, creasing along the bisector EC of the angle BCD, fold to the left (Fig. 3). This brings BC onto DC, or vertical, and B is at the maximum distance from the book's edge. (The book can now be shut, folding the page on BC.)

(All books shown open)

Continued on next page

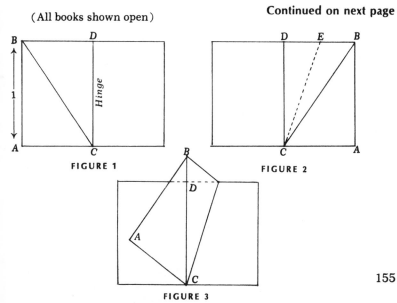

FIGURE 1

FIGURE 2

FIGURE 3

155

If the book were sufficiently wider in proportion to height, A would be above the top edge (Fig. 4), but we are told an outer corner is *on* an edge, and since B is above it, A is on the top edge (Fig. 5).

Proof: (Figure 5 is labeled as shown)

[By a well-known theorem] Since BAC and BDA are right angles, AD is the "mean proportional" of BD and DC, or $x : y = y : 1$,

∴ $x/y = y/1$

∴ $y^2 = x$

By Pythagoras, $y^2 + x^2 = 1$

∴ $x + x^2 = 1$, and since $x = d - 1$

$d - 1 + (d - 1)^2 = 1$

∴ $d - 1 + d^2 - 2d + 1 = 1$

∴ $d^2 - d = 1$

∴ $d + 1 = d^2$, from which we can see that

$d = \phi$, or $1.618\ldots$

∴ $x = \phi - 1$

Q.E.D.

(All books shown open)

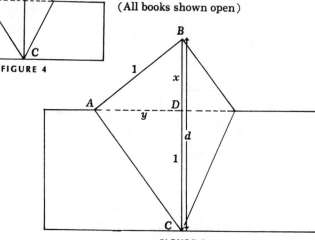

FIGURE 4

FIGURE 5

156

SNOW ON THE ROOF

Just over 2 ft. $(1 + \sqrt{2}$ times 10 in., or 24.142
... in.).

The figure shows a cross section of the roof
and snow, thicker on the right (west) than the
left (east), which measures 10 in. The direction of the snowfall (dotted line) is obviously
the bisector of the angle between the roof and
level ground, since equal thicknesses of snow
were on them. Since the sides of the roof are at
45° to the level, the diagram can be labeled as
shown, and since c bisects $2\,\alpha$, triangles 1 and
2 are congruent.

From this we can see that $a\sqrt{2} + a = b$;
and if $a = 10$ in.; then $b = (\sqrt{2} + 1) \times 10 =$
24.142. . . . (Even if the wind were not due
west, we could get the same result by considering its westerly component, only.)

$a =$ thickness of snow on east slope $= 10$ in.
$b =$ ditto on west slope

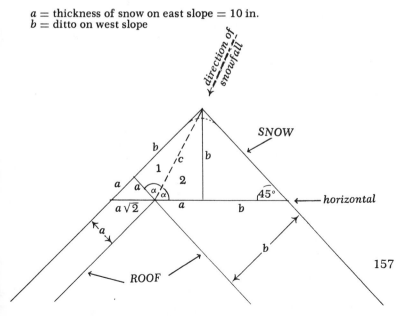

34

DRAFTING PUZZLE

He has a sheet of ruled paper.

He puts the compass point at any point C on any line, e.g., 1, and sets the radius to line 3 beyond line 2 (next to C) and draws a circle which touches 3 at D, and line 5 at G, and cuts 2 at A and E, and 4 at B and F. A, D, E, F, G, and B are the required vertices of a hexagon.

Proof: Radius $AC = $ radius $BC = AB = DC$; thus ABC is an equilateral triangle. For the same reason EFC is an equilateral triangle, and opposite to ABC. Thus A, E, F, and B are vertices of a hexagon, and, since by symmetry D and G are the midpoints of arcs AE and FB, respectively, they too are vertices of the hexagon.

Q.E.D.

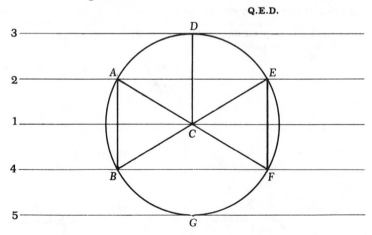

THE PSYCHEDELIC CUBE

The model will be of three slightly distorted, contiguous faces of a cube, but the *surface* to be looked at is the inside (Fig. 1).

The orthogonal projection of a cube seen from a corner is a regular hexagon with three radial edges meeting at that corner, A (Fig. 2). As can be seen, the projection could just as well be of the inside view, like Fig. 1 seen from the same angle but turned 60° on its axis (the line of sight), to bring one of the rhombuses to the top, in which case A would be the furthest point, E, instead of the nearest. (Figure 3 shows that three radial edges of a cube seen from that angle, compared with the corresponding radial edges of the model before turning it on its axis, to demonstrate the necessity of so doing.)

Continued on next page

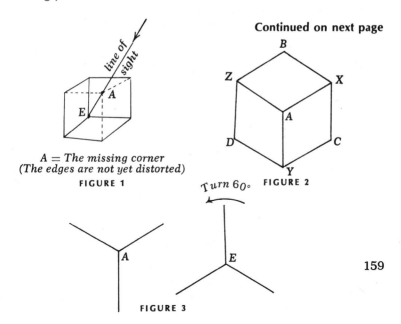

$A =$ *The missing corner*
(The edges are not yet distorted)
FIGURE 1

Turn 60°   **FIGURE 2**

FIGURE 3

159

Perspective projection would not be so ambiguous; the dotted lines, Fig. 4, show how the three corners, B, C, and D would be pulled in toward the center A. If this same projection were of the model (Fig. 1), the corners X', Y', and Z' would be pulled in (Fig. 5), provided we have turned it 60° to bring the radial edges AX', AY', and AZ' into alignment with the ones in Fig. 4. If we now project the dotted lines from Fig. 4 onto Fig. 5 and cut along them, we get Fig. 6, which will then look like the corner view of a (convex) cube, and is what we want. Notice that we make use of the three radial edges, but they now masquerade as *convex* edges, and the center point E, the far corner, will appear to be the nearest. Since the projected figures are symmetrical, we shall consider only one face, $BXAZ$, which is the top of the cube we shall think we are seeing. Figure 7 shows the method of perspective projection of the face $BXAZ$, in plan and from the side, onto $B'X'EZ'$.

$A =$ *the missing corner. (The edges are not yet distorted.)*

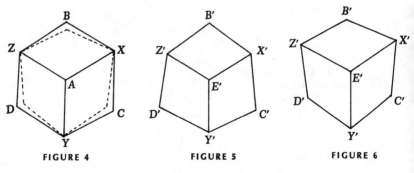

FIGURE 4   FIGURE 5   FIGURE 6

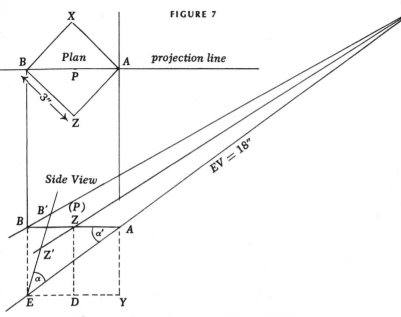

FIGURE 7

$\angle \alpha = \angle \alpha'$ because that is the angle of face $B'X'A'Z'$ of the model when in the position relative to EV that gives the view shown in Fig. 5.

V is the projection point, or eye, and a reasonable viewing distance is 18 in. The imaginary cube, with top $BXAZ$, should be about 3 in. wide. In actuality all we need to establish is the diagonal AB, with its center point P (coincident with Z in the projection). We then lay out the quadrilateral $B'X'E'Z'$ on cardboard, with $X'E'Z'$ a right angle; cut three pieces that size and shape, and join them as shown (Fig. 8). When the two edges $Z'E$ are pulled together we get Fig. 1, but with a modified (or distorted) outer edge.

Continued on next page

35   **Continued**

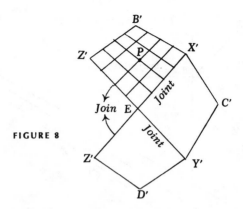

FIGURE 8

It is best not to make the construction from one piece shaped like Fig. 8, because one cannot make a very sharp fold in cardboard. Join the pieces edges to edge with tape on the back, and blacken the outer edges, otherwise they look too light—they represent edges that turn *away* from us. The effect is heightened if we draw a grid of crossed lines in the appropriate perspective on at least one face, as in Fig. 8, top face. The end points of these lines can be got in the projection by making equal subdivisions on *AZB*, and marking them off on *E'Z'B'* in the same way we established the points *E'Z'B'*. Using this grid we can lay out designs or lettering too by drawing them first on a rectangular grid and then transferring, point by point.

The model should be taken up and held perfectly still, with both eyes closed. Then open *one* eye. Afterward the model can be slightly turned; the effect is quite odd. It is best done out of doors, not in the direct sunlight; otherwise the shadows will be in the wrong places.

CONSTRUCTION PROBLEM

Since the stairs are of equal width, the space occupied by a turn is a square, one corner of which touches the diagonal *AB*. With *M* the midpoint of *AE*, draw the line *MN* parallel to *AF*. Draw *MP* with *PN* = ½ *MN*; the intersection, *I*, gives the corner of one of the equal bins, dotted.

Proof:
MN is the line joining the center point of the top of a square, with *PN* as half its base; therefore *MP* is the locus of the corners of squares, the center point of whose tops is *M*, such as the required square *XYZI*.

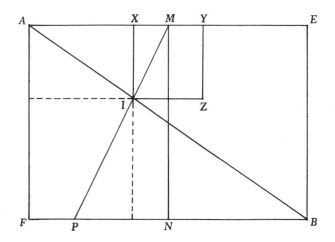

37

A WALK IN A FIELD

16 rd.

As the diagram shows, each segment walked is one of the equal sides of an isosceles right triangle, and the formula can be easily found by inspection: $d = \sqrt{2^n}$; in this case $n = 8$, $2^8 = 256$; $\sqrt{256} = 16$.

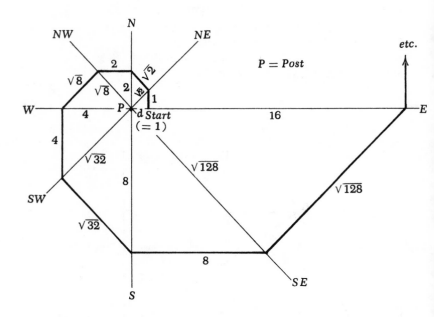

Answer 2

The following will be readily understood by plotting his walk on squared paper, as in the figure. Each square has side $= 1$, and diagonal $= \sqrt{2}$. First he walks one side, and then one diagonal; then two sides and two diagonals; then four sides and four diagonals; etc. Thus the formula for even numbers of n is $d = 2^{\frac{n}{2}}$; and for odd numbers of n, $d = (n-1)\sqrt{2}$. In the first case the man multiplies 2 by itself, half the number of segments walked; in the second, or odd-number, cases, all he has to remember is $\sqrt{2}$ (1.4142, etc.) as far as the table would, and multiply it by the number of segments minus 1. The latter formula applies also to an even-number n, but the results cannot be worked out without tables—or a phenomenal memory.

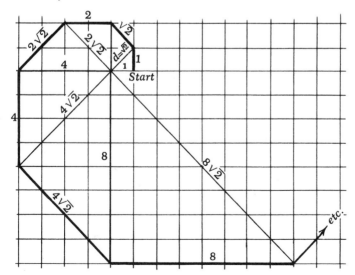

38

MORE DIAGONALS

When $w = 1$, $l = l^3 - 1$ (approx. 1.325).
All angles marked α are complements of angle β.

By similar triangles 1 and 2:
$$c/a = a/b; \therefore c = a^2/b$$

By similar triangles 2 and 3:
$$\frac{a}{b} = \frac{b}{a + c}, \therefore a^2 + ac = b^2,$$
$$\therefore ac = b^2 - a^2$$

Substitute for c:
$$a^3/b = b^2 - a^2, \therefore a^3 = b^3 - a^2b,$$
$$\therefore a^2b = b^3 - a^3$$

Divide both sides by a^3:
$$\text{thus } b/a = (b/a)^3 - 1$$

By similar triangles:
$$l/w = b/a, \text{ and } w = 1$$
$$\therefore l = b/a$$
$$\therefore l = l^3 - 1$$

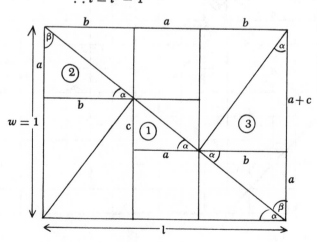

SHORT PROOF (CUT CUBE)

Any two parallel equilateral triangles, whose vertices lie at vertices of the cube, trisect the interior diagonal of the cube which is perpendicular to them.

Proof:

(The figure we use is an orthogonal view of the cube shown in Fig. 1, from the direction of the arrow, so that the line of sight is parallel to the diagonals *AC* and *EG*. The two triangles mentioned above are *ACH* and *BGE*, and the orthogonal view is shown in Fig. 2, with the same lettering, and with three added lines.)

Since all the edges are equal, and all angles right angles, except for diagonals; by symmetry, the four triangles labeled 1, 2, 3, and 4 are congruent. Therefore their altitudes are equal, and the diagonal *FD* is trisected by the parallel lines *CH* and *BG*.

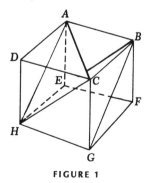

FIGURE 1

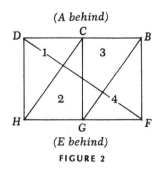

FIGURE 2

40

WORD CHANGING

ASK
ARK
ART
AIT
WIT
WAT
WAY
WHY

(*note*: WAT is given in many
dictionaries: var. of WET, Scot., or of
WOT)

Answer 2

SPRING
SPYING
SAYING
SAVING
CAVING
CANING
CONING
CONINS
CONIES
COPIES
COPIER
COPPER
CAPPER
CARPER
CARDER
WARDER
WANDER
WINDER
WINTER

(*note:* CONIN is a var. spelling of
what killed Socrates)

POLYHEDRAL MODEL

90°.

Answer 2

A cube.

The first answer is most easily got if we answer the second question. We think of the central hexagon as the hexagonal plane which bisects a cube (Fig. 1): Its vertices are the numbered midpoints of six of the cube's edges; consequently we can draw lines of equal length from these vertices to the corners *A* and *B* of the cube. These lines form twelve edges of a semiregular, twelve-faced polyhedron; its remaining six edges are the hexagon, and all the triangular faces are congruent. Figure 2 shows one face on a side of the cube; its altitude is one and a half times its base, which enables us to identify our model with this particular polyhedron, whose alternate sides are parts of the faces of a cube, and thus at 90° with one another.

Shaded △s on the far sides ∼
Hexagonal plane omitted.

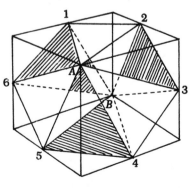

FIGURE 1

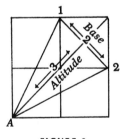

FIGURE 2

169

42

DIHEDRAL ANGLES

We draw the additional lines shown, with O as center of the hexagon, IJ and HK as perpendicular bisectors of EG and GF respectively. By symmetry, $IH = 3$, and $BG = CG = 2$. We extend the triangles AEB and CFD to form the larger triangles AEG and DFG; then when E and F are brought together by folding at AG and DG, the edges EG and FG coincide, and J meets K, forming a new triangle, $I(JK)H$. If we now call the length IG, 1 $(= HG = IE = FH)$, then $JI = KH = \sqrt{2}/2$; therefore in the triangle thus formed, the angle $I(JK)H$ is a right angle. Since IJ and KH are both at right angles to the common edge of the two triangles in question, the dihedral angle between them is a right angle, and consequently between the triangles AEB and CFD.

Q.E.D.

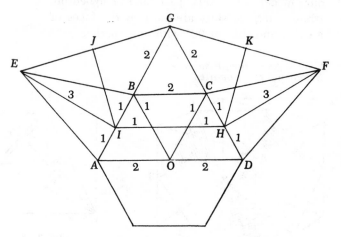

CHEESE WEDGES

$w = 1$; $l = \sqrt{2}$; $h = \sqrt{2}/3$ (Fig. 1).

We start with Mrs. H's method: Figure 2 shows the diagrammatic cross section of the wedge with cuts; the beveled edges fit together in pairs, so the number of slices is always even. With two slices (one cut), the plan is unchanged, but Mrs. H said it was "too small," so she must have made more slices. It will be seen that with four slices w is doubled, the expression being that if n is the number of slices, and x is the total width of adjoining slices—the single row she spoke of—then $x = nw/2$. With four slices, if the proportions are to remain the same, she must do it by reversing l with w, as it were (Fig. 3). Then the equation is with $w = 1$, $l = 2/l$, $\therefore l^2 = 2$, or $l = \sqrt{2}$; so the bread measures $\sqrt{2}$ by 2, $(2/\sqrt{2} = \sqrt{2})$, which we see is not an unusual proportion for bread.

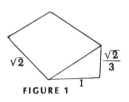

FIGURE 1

Continued on next page

FIGURE 2

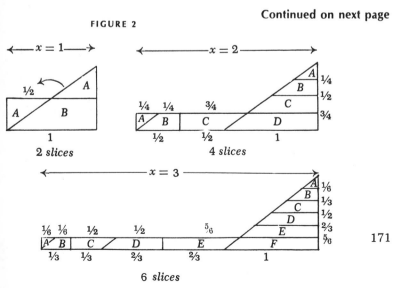

2 slices

4 slices

6 slices

171

43 Continued

If she had made six slices ($x = 3$; Fig. 2), a similar equation for unaltered proportions gives $l = \sqrt{3}$. Yet as we see in Fig. 4, that would be abnormally tall for a loaf, and the greater we make n, the worse it gets; therefore she made four slices, and the plan of the cheese wedges was 1 by $\sqrt{2}$.

For the height, h, we turn to Mrs. V's method: here again the slices must go in pairs (Fig. 5). Since the bread measures $\sqrt{2}$ by 2, she must have arranged her slices in at least two rows (Fig. 6), but she made "almost four times as many cuts" as Mrs. H, so the arrangement must have been as in Fig. 7, or twelve slices— eleven cuts is almost four times three cuts. Obviously the number of slices for Mrs. V is always

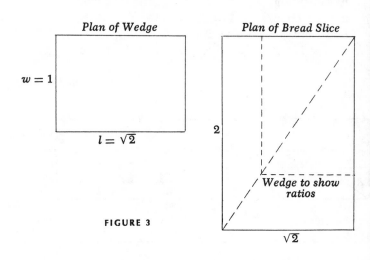

Plan of Wedge

$w = 1$

$l = \sqrt{2}$

FIGURE 3

Plan of Bread Slice

2

$\sqrt{2}$

Wedge to show ratios

a multiple of four, and eight slices would only need seven cuts. From this we see her slices were $l/12$ in thickness, and since both ladies dealt with the same volume of cheese, $h = 4/12\ l$, or $\sqrt{2}/3$.

We can be thankful that Mrs. H did not arrange her slices in more than one row, because it leads to boring complications.

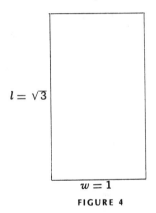

FIGURE 4

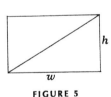

FIGURE 5

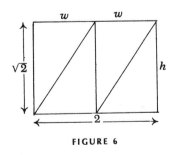

FIGURE 6

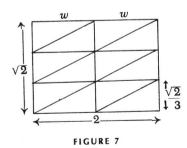

FIGURE 7

44

THE POISONED GLASS

129.

The normal, most efficient procedure, is to test half the glasses together, then half of whichever group is shown to be poisoned, then half again, etc., until the guilty glass is found. Thus the powers of 2 give the first clue: For two glasses we need one test; for three or four we need two tests; for five to eight we need three tests; and so on. 128 is the only power of 2 between 100 and 200, so for 129 and up, we need 8 tests. That is to say, we *may* need 8; but in testing 1 first, the remaining 128 need only 7 tests, so that in whole-number chances there is no difference.

Actually there is an expectancy of 7.0155 . . . tests when using the halving procedure, but of 7.9457 . . . when testing a single one first, thus wasting .930 . . . of a test—as the professor said, "Not quite a whole test." (His gamble paid off, it was the first glass, which strained the credulity of the lab technician so that he went ahead and tested them all.)

TO COVER A CIRCLE

The solid lines (Fig. 1) show the original rectangle. She establishes the center point, O, with two creases, and then divides the bottom edge successively into 1/4 (the first crease has given the 1/2), 1/8, 1/16, and 1/32, and folds along a line FF' through O, and tilted so that the 1/32 mark, A, lies on the top edge. (O is later used for finding the center of the required maximum circle.) The dotted lines show the new position.

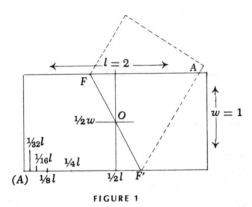

FIGURE 1

Proof:

Figure 2 is drawn to the proportions given, but we ignore the fact that the length is 2, and call it l. O is the center of the unfolded rectangle, and the folded shape is symmetrical about AO, perpendicular to FF', the fold. D, the center of the required circle, which is tangent to FF' at O, and to the ends of the paper $A'E$ (taking

Continued on next page

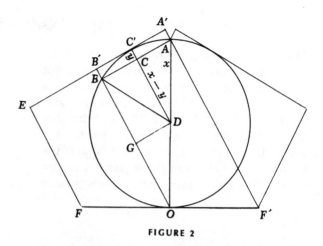

FIGURE 2

only one because the shape is symmetrical) at C′, and passing through A, the intersection of the long edges.

DC′ is perpendicular to A′E; draw OB′ perpendicular to A′E, and thus parallel to DC′ and FE. O is the center of FF′, therefore B′ is the center of A′E. Draw a line from A to B, the intersection of OB′ with the required circle; then ∠ABO is a right angle because it is in a semicircle; therefore AB is parallel to A′B′. Draw BD; since ∠ACD is a right angle, AC = CB; therefore AC = 1/4.

Draw DG perpendicular to OB; then OG = BG = CD. B′O = l/2; let x = radius AD, and y = l/2 − 2 BG. BG = CD = x −y;

∴ y = l/2 − 2x + 2y

∴ y = 2x − l/2 or 2x − y = l/2 (Equation 1)

In the right triangle ACD, the sides are x, x − y, and 1/4;

$\therefore x^2 = x^2 - 2\,xy + y^2 + 1/16$

$\therefore 2\,xy - y^2 = 1/16$ (Equation 2)

Multiply both sides of Equation 1 by y;

$2\,xy - y^2 = yl/2$; then with Equation 2 we get

$yl/2 = 1/16$

$y = \frac{1}{8}l$

This was the value Suzi calculated for AA', with $l = 2$; $AA' = 1/16$. The circle covered has radius $= l/4 + y/2$, in this case $1/32$ more than the circle covered by the unfolded paper.

Answer 2

$$l_1 = \frac{1}{4 - 2\sqrt{3}} \text{ and } l_2 = \frac{1}{6 - 2\sqrt{8}}$$

The lower limit, l_1, is when the required circle has a diameter of 1, the width of the paper, giving no advantage. The upper limit, l_2 which gives the greatest advantage, is when the circle touches the long edges of the paper. Any further increase of l_2 means that the circle calculated by the above method will be too big to be covered.

Continued on next page

45 Continued

In the first case (Fig. 1), $x = w/2$, or $1/2$, so that in the $\triangle ADC$, $DA = 2/4$ and $AC = 1/4$; $\therefore DC = \sqrt{3}/4 = 1/2 - y$; $y = 1/2 - \sqrt{3}/4 = \dfrac{2 - \sqrt{3}}{4}$. $y = \frac{1}{8}l$; $\therefore l = \dfrac{1}{4 - 2\sqrt{3}}$

Q.E.D.

The upper limit (Fig. 2; showing the left half only) gives $x = 3/4$ because $CE = 3/4$; so in $\triangle ADC$, $DA = 3/4$ and $AC = 1/4$; $\therefore DC = \dfrac{\sqrt{8}}{4} = \dfrac{3}{4} - y$, $y = \dfrac{1}{8l}$, $\therefore \dfrac{3 - \sqrt{8}}{4} = \dfrac{1}{8l}$; $\therefore l = \dfrac{1}{6 - 2\sqrt{8}}$

Q.E.D.

Asymmetrical folding, where FF' does not go through O, within rather narrow limits can give slightly higher values for x, but is too unwieldy to discuss here, and comes under the heading of problems rather than puzzles.

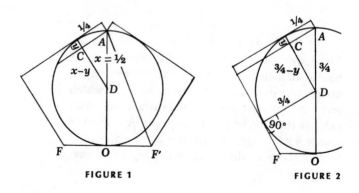

FIGURE 1　　　　　　　　FIGURE 2

It is diophantine; that is, the ratio of its sides is rational, and can be reduced to finite whole numbers. In the case given, with $w = 1$, $l = 2$, the $\triangle ADC$ has sides measuring $1/4$, $x - y$, and x. $y = 1/16$; $x = l/4 - y/2 = 1/2 - 1/32$; so the three sides are $1/4$, $17/32 - 1/16$, and $17/32$. Reduced to the same denominator, $8/32$, $15/32$, and $17/32$, and $8^2 - 15^2 = 17^2$. If $l = w$, the sides are 3, 4, and 5. Since we can always express a rational w/l by reducing w to 1, the general formula for the sides of the triangle in question is: where l is a rational number, the sides are as l, $l^2 - 1/4$, and $l^2 + 1/4$. This is another version of the more usual expression:

> If n is an odd number, the sides are n, $1/2(n^2 - 1)$, $1/2(n^2 + 1)$,
>
> If n is a whole number, the sides are n, $(n/2)^2 - 1$, $(n/2)^2 + 1$.

In this way any proportion of rectangle that can be established by folding (i.e., that is obtainable by the feasible subdivisions; all the powers of 2, and a wide variety of others) allows one to mark off y on the edge, and thus fold the optimum shape within the limits given above for symmetrical folding.

46

PURE ORIGAMI SOLUTION

In Fig. 1 the creases are numbered in order. 1, 2, and 3 are successive halvings of the width, 1, giving $AC = 1/8$. Crease 4 runs from C to the corner, B (must be very exact). 5 brings the edge BD up to coincide with the top edge AB, enabling one to mark the length y with crease 6 on the bottom edge next to D. With some finagling (Fig. 2), the y at D is transferred to the top edge next to A, with crease 7. The final fold, 8, dotted, is made by bringing D up and over next to A, and adjusting until creases 6 and 7 just meet—and flattening carefully.

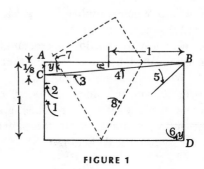

FIGURE 1

Proof:

In Fig. 1, AB is to $AC(1/8)$ as 1 is to y, being in similar triangles. Thus $\frac{l}{1/8} = \frac{1}{y}$; $y = \frac{1/8}{l} = \frac{1}{8l}$, which is the required value, as proved in Puzzle 45.

Suzi explained to Lillian that it also works for rectangles shorter than the low limit—even a square—but that no advantage is gained in size of circle covered. "I shouldn't have brought up all this math," she said. "I know you're not keen on it."

"Mathematics, no," replied Lillian, "mathematicians, yes. Anyway I like the shape it makes: I expect it to fold its wings like the scarab, and as busily buzz away."

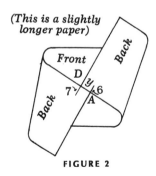

FIGURE 2

47

THE FLAT PAN

He fills the pan on the table more than half-full, and then carefully tilts up one end, pouring out the water, until the level reaches *E*, the bottom edge of the raised end (Fig. 1). This leaves exactly 1/2 pt. in the pan, since the empty part is the same shape and size as the filled part.

Being an ordinary kitchen type, the table has a straight edge; the man slides the pan over the edge so that the opposite corners, *C* and *C'*, coincide with the edge (Fig. 2), and starts tilting again, with the bowl held to catch the water. He tilts until the surface of the water coincides with the corners *C* and *C'*. The bowl now contains 1/3 pt.

Proof:

Proportions of the pan are ignored. Figure 3 shows the pan at the end of pouring. The remaining water is in the form of a pyramid, the volume of which equals the area of the base times one-third its height. Here the area of base

$$= \frac{lw}{2} \therefore \text{volume} = \frac{lw}{2} \times \frac{h}{3} = \frac{lwh}{6}.$$

Since the volume of the pan (1 pt.) = lwh, the remaining water = 1/6 pt.

Thus he poured into the bowl 1/2 − 1/6 pt.; or 1/3 pt.

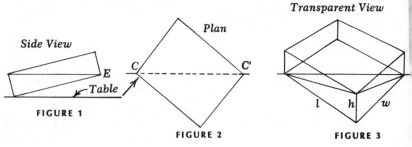

Side View

E

Table

FIGURE 1

Plan

C — — — — — — — *C'*

FIGURE 2

Transparent View

l   *h*   *w*

FIGURE 3

THE SIAMESE MOEBIUS STRIP

One piece, two sides, three edges (1, 2, and 3), no twists, topologically speaking, for the twists in the upper part are canceled out by those in the lower. There are also two holes.

The answer was foreseeable (see Fig. 2), since *EB*, the lower edge of *L*, joins *B'A*, the upper edge of *R* and *L*, which joins *A'E'*, the lower edge of *R*; then *EBB'AA'E'* together make the upper half of edge one (Fig. 1). The lower half of edge one is formed analogously by *FCC'DD'F'*.

The inner edge made by cut *X* (dotted), and the outer edge made by cut *Y*, together make edge three (Fig. 1), and analogously the outer edge *X* and the inner edge *Y* make edge two (Fig. 1). This tells us there are three edges. By following the connections made by the joints, we see that the strip remains in one piece.

Finally, in each case a twisted element is joined to one twisted oppositely; therefore all twists cancel; therefore there are (topologically) no twists, and from that we see there must be two sides, as there were before joining and cutting.

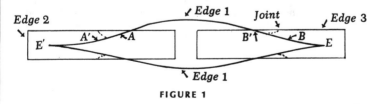

FIGURE 1

FIGURE 2

49

THE NINE DIGITS

The first line is produced by multiplying the nine digits in their natural order, by three, and writing down the final digits of the products; the second is produced by multiplying the digits by seven, and writing the terminal digits of the products.

When one and nine are used as the multipliers we again get all nine digits, but in natural and reversed order, respectively. The other digits give less than all nine digits. This leads to zeros and repeats, which throws everything off (see figure).

Multipliers	Terminal Digits*
1	123456789
2	246802468
3	369258147
4	482604826
5	505050505
6	628406284
7	741852963
8	864208642
9	987654321

*With operation X the first and last of these produce themselves. It will be noticed that the pattern formed by this figure is like a word square, in that it reads the same down as across.

MINIMUM AREA

Figure 1 shows one way to start; the sides add up to 4s, and the area is reduced to $5/9s^2$. But if we try to improve it by reducing the length of the sides, and increasing their number (Fig. 2), getting an area of $41/81s^2$, and continue to increase the number of sides, we can see that the limit is area $= \frac{1}{2}s^2$.

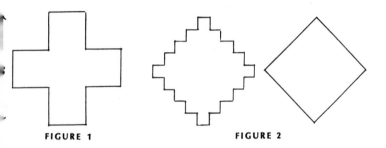

FIGURE 1   FIGURE 2

One solution—there are others, but more complicated—is Fig. 3. Figure 4 shows the method carried further, and Fig. 5 shows the limit, with zero area. The latter would, of course, have to be reduced the appropriate amount, like the others, to give the right length of sides, in this case by one-half, because they are still twice as long as they look, due to the (now) infinitely small and infinitely numerous

Continued on next page

steps. Topologically the solutions just described form an open set, for the *limit* case is excluded since by definition the sides would be touching one another, the distance between them being zero. This does not affect the answer, however.

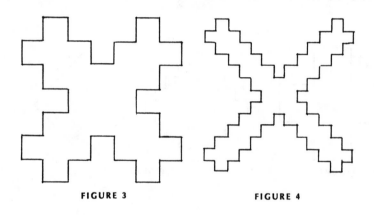

FIGURE 3   FIGURE 4

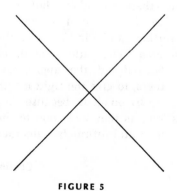

FIGURE 5

COCYCLIC POINTS

The four points of intersection of circle E, which needs no proof, and the points A, B, C, and D.

Proof:
A and C are right angles; draw DB, which we consider to be the diameter of an imaginary circle. Any point, such as A or C, subtended at a right angle by D and B, will lie on the circle.

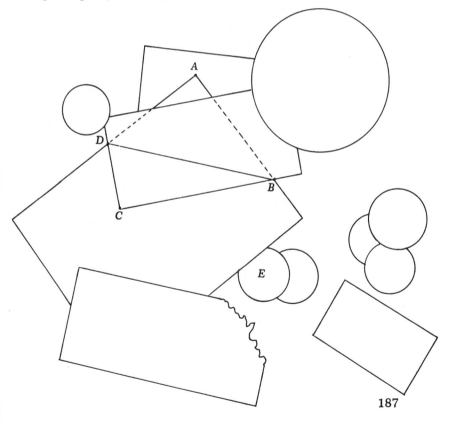

52

THE TILTED CARTON

Enough milk to fill the carton to a depth of half its width, or less; $\alpha = 45°$. This is true for any proportion of carton if $h > w$. If $h = w$, the amount of milk has no effect on α.

Proof:

Figure 1 shows the carton tilted to $\alpha = 45°$. C is the midpoint of the dotted line parallel to the base AB, and at a distance of $\frac{1}{2}w$ from it; when the carton is tilted, the level of the milk will still pass through C, and at 45° will also touch B. Symmetry shows the carton will balance at this angle (ignoring the weight of the carton). If any more milk is added, NN', the extra milk will be off-center to the left, so that the new center of gravity will be to the left of the vertical axis CA, and the carton will tip. If on the other hand the amount of milk is *less*, the center of gravity will still be vertically above A when $\alpha = 45°$.

When $h = w$ the carton may be full, partially full or empty, and α will always be 45°. If $h < w$, any amount of milk less than full reduces α.

TOPOLOGY PUZZLE

As shown in Fig. 1. The edges can be followed by eye for counting. The rule is that the number of holes is unlimited provided it is odd. Figure 2 shows an uncompleted model with three holes and the possibility of a fourth if we join the loose end to x. If the joint is made *without* a twist, we shall have four holes and two edges but only one side; *with* a twist we shall have two sides and four holes, but three edges. This applies to all even numbers of holes.

Shaded part is the second side

Twists may be in either direction

FIGURE 1

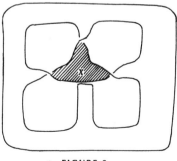

FIGURE 2

189

54

THE VANADIUM STEEL CLOTHESLINE

We first prove that the folding produces another rectangle. In Fig. 1, $\angle BCE = \angle ECD$. Since AB is folded to lie on CB, FB bisects $\angle ABC$, which equals $\angle BCD$; $\therefore$ FB is parallel to CE.

In Fig. 2, G is the new position of A; $\angle FGB = 90°$. C is next folded over so that CF lies on FG; thus the fold, FH, bisects $\angle CFG$. $\angle HFG = \frac{1}{2}CFG$, and $\angle BFG = \frac{1}{2}\angle AFG$; $\therefore$ $\angle BFH = 90°$. By symmetry $\angle FJK = 90°$; $\therefore$ $FJKH$ is a rectangle. (Also CH will lie on OH.)

We shall call the length and width of the cloth l and w, and the proportion of the final rectangle, $R = \frac{2x}{y}$ (Fig. 3). We draw a line from B, parallel with the ends (w), and label certain angles α and β, which have been proved or are obvious, with α the same as in Fig. 1, and β the complement of α. Then by similar triangles: $\frac{2y}{w} = \frac{2a}{l}$, $\therefore$ $a = \frac{ly}{w}$. Also $\frac{2y}{l-2b} = \frac{2a}{w} = \frac{2ly}{w^2}$, $\therefore$ $l - 2b = \frac{w^2}{l}$.

By similar triangles, $\frac{x}{b} = \frac{2y}{w}$, $\therefore$ $b = \frac{xw}{2y}$. Since $R = \frac{2x}{y}$, $x = \frac{Ry}{2}$; substitute $\frac{Rw}{2}$ for x, getting $b = \frac{Ry}{2} - \frac{w}{2y} = \frac{Rw}{4}$. Substitute for b: $l - 2b = l - \frac{Rw}{2}$. By similar triangles: $\frac{l-2b}{w} = \frac{w}{l}$,

$$\therefore l - \frac{Rw}{2} = \frac{w^2}{l}, \therefore l - \frac{w^2}{l} = \frac{Rw}{2}.$$

So with $w = 1$, $R = 2l - \frac{2}{l}$. With this expression for R, we can get the answers. First the red tablecloth: the professor said its proportions were the same as the folded rectangle's. That is,

$R = l$. Then $l = \dfrac{2l^2 - 2}{l}$, and $l^2 = 2l^2 - 2$, or $l = \sqrt{2}$.

Then the ϕ-proportion tablecloth: $\phi = \dfrac{\sqrt{5} + 1}{2}$, but it is simpler to use another expression, $\phi^2 = \phi + 1$. From this we get

$R = 2\phi - \dfrac{2}{\phi} = \dfrac{2\phi^2 - 2}{\phi} = \dfrac{2\phi}{\phi} = 2.$

The reader may care to experiment with other proportions of the cloth, or R. A surprising number of them lead to diophantine solutions, and Mrs. M's tablecloths got all dirty.

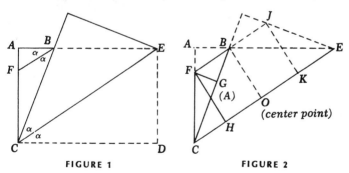

FIGURE 1   FIGURE 2

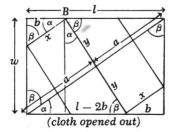

(cloth opened out)

FIGURE 3

191

55

VISUALIZING

A black-on-white, square spiral, going inward *clockwise*.

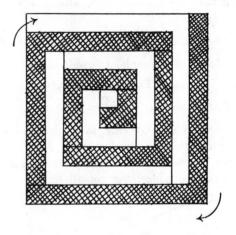

THE BALANCE

The scale is straight, and moves with the balance. It is attached at a distance, c, from F, and at right angles to a line radial to F (Fig. 1), and the graduations are equally spaced. The fixed vertical line V acts as a pointer to show the weight of L on the scale, as a distance on it, a. Figure 2 shows a state of equilibrium, in which L and W are the downward forces of the load and weight (W is constant) as before; b is the distance of L from F, and a the distance of W from F; so again $xL = yW$. Since VF is

Continued on next page

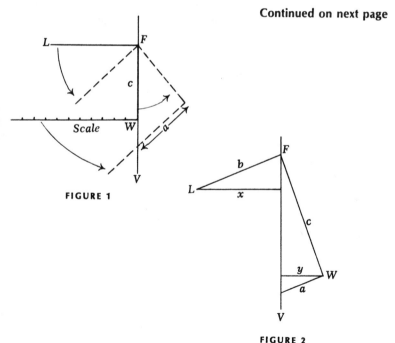

FIGURE 1

FIGURE 2

56 ^{Continued}

vertical, and a and b are parallel, all the triangles are similar:

$$\therefore a/b = y/x$$
$$\therefore ax = by$$

From before, $x = \dfrac{yW}{L}$

Substitute for x, $\dfrac{ayW}{L} = by$

$$\therefore a = \frac{Lb}{W}$$

Since b and W are constant when L changes, a is changed proportionally; e.g., if we double L, then $\dfrac{2Lb}{W} = 2a$, etc. It will be noticed that c need not equal b. There are many other arrangements of the scale which embody the above principle.

HYDRAULIC INFERENCE

A squat cylinder; approximately 5 by 8. (The old style of coffee cans would be very near, both in proportion and size.)

Most, if not all, thin kitchen pots are round. It was stated that the water, after stopping, continued to rise at *exactly* half its previous rate, which strongly implies that its previous rate was constant; therefore its sides were vertical. Since the first rate was twice that of the second, the pot's area of cross section was half that of the cubical casserole, and the pot's height is of course half. Taking the width of the casserole as 2, the radius, r, of the pot is got from $\pi r^2 = 2$ (half the area of the casserole); therefore $r = \sqrt{2/\pi}$, almost .8, as shown in the figure. (The actual capacity of the casserole is not needed for the above.)

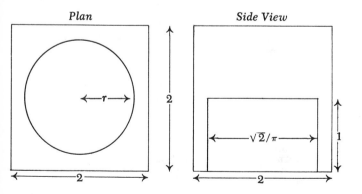

Plan   Side View

58

THE STRIPED WHATSIS

It is a solid, not a strip, and best described as a torus with a triangular cross section and one complete twist. Thus it has three faces and three edges. At first glance one might take it for a Moebius strip with three half-twists, which, like the usual one-half twist Moebius strip, has one side and one edge, but when examined more closely, we see that something funny is going on.

For one thing it is obvious that the edge AA' is not part of the edge CC', but by no stretch of visual imagination can the edge BB' be considered as a continuation of AA'. We can, in fact, count three disconnected edges. Also, the light and dark bands are an anomaly, for they suggest a non-existent parallelism, as between edges BB' and CC' (Fig. 1). Figure 2 shows the three edges, each a circle, and Fig. 3 shows one of the three identical surfaces cut out and laid flat. It is the latter that shows us how far from parallel the edges are, and how arbitrary and misleading the light and dark bands.

A model can be made by cutting the three surfaces from cardboard, and assembling and joining the edges—it is quite hard to manage but rather pretty.*

*Note to model maker: since the surfaces are warped, and cannot be opened out to a true flat plane, the cardboard must be thin, and soaked in water so that it will stretch.

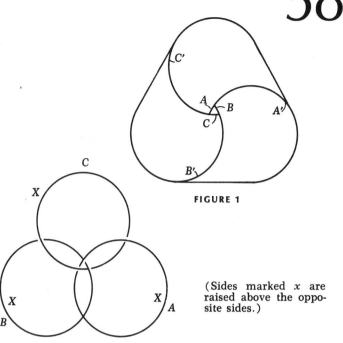

FIGURE 1

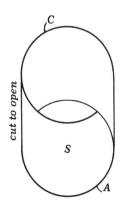

FIGURE 2

(Sides marked *x* are raised above the opposite sides.)

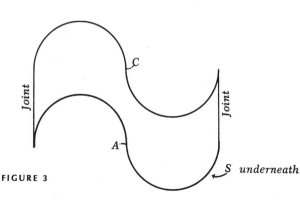

FIGURE 3

The 2-sided surface with edges *A* and *C*. *S* is the *inside* and concealed by solid.

The same surface opened out flat.

THE TERRI TURNOVER

It can, and there is no difference in appearance. It all depends on the shape and material.

Mrs. Terri Burkhardt sent to this writer a Klein bottle—an incredible achievement: it was knitted in red wool! Its proportions were as shown here, topologically the equal of the model shown in the question (the latter always seems to be made of glass—they *say*). As we see, the transformation leads to an end result that is the same as before, but the label, *L*, sewn on the outside, so to speak, is now on the hidden part of the surface.

This transformation is far more surprising than the inverted torus, in that the shape is unaltered.

Terri Turnover

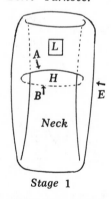 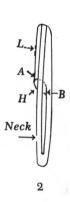 

Stage 1	2	3
Made from a cylinder, but being wool it lies flat. *A* and *B* are parts of edge of hole *H*. *L* is a label. *H* is moved up, neck down.	View from edge *E*; *H* is moved up and neck down.	Front view: *L* has just disappeared over the top, inside. *H* is almost at the top.

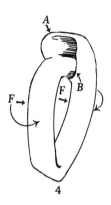

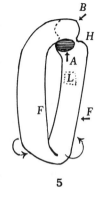

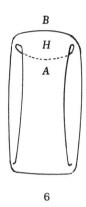

| 4 | 5 | 6 |

Turned more than stage 2, to show back as *H* has reached top. Back edges *FF* now twisted to front, and

Reversing the positions of *A* and *B*. Part of *H* faces away,

Now turned all the way, we see the back, and start to roll *B* down,

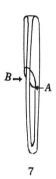

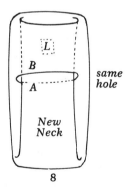

| 7 | 8 |

Over what is now the front (edge view again),

Ending with this, which is to all appearances the same as stage 1.

Continued on next page

59 Continued

Answer 2

Square when flattened, or cut and opened out flat (Fig. 1). The material may be rubber (or better, knitted wool). Its torus form will not be immediately apparent when flat, but as the sequential diagrams show (Fig. 2), inversion changes length for width, so equality of these will insure an unchanged proportion of the torus. The hole should run the full half-width, as with the Terri Turnover, for ease of inverting, but is shown here stretched still more.

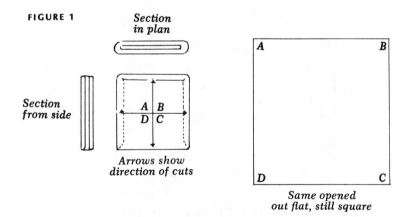

FIGURE 1

Section in plan

Section from side

A B
D C

Arrows show direction of cuts

A   B

D   C

Same opened out flat, still square

FIGURE 2

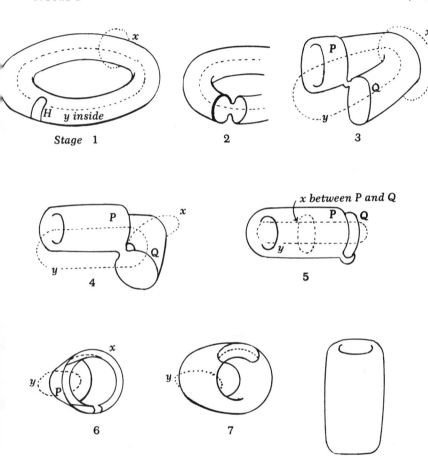

Stage 1

2

3

4

x between P and Q

5

6

7

8

1. Normal proportion. 2. We begin to stretch the hole until it leaves only a narrow connection: then we begin. 3. To roll part of the torus back on itself like a stocking, labeling the newly appeared part of the inner surface P, and the outer Q. 4. Then we continue as shown. 5. Until P is back next to Q. 6. And reduce the hole to 7. Its original shape. 8. Turned into the original position.

THE HEAVY CHEST

Figure 1 (page 82) shows each stage, four moves in all.

Answer 2

As shown in the figure. (This can be made into a board game.)

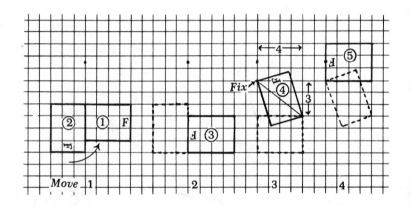

The diagonal,
thin line, reaches
the corner (Fix)
of a 3 x 4 rect.

THE PILE AND THE PATRIOT

Start with the triangular arrangement—like his second, but the outline of the first layer is a hexagon (irregular) (Fig. 1). The second layer goes on the S' squinches, but the third layer goes *directly over the first*, which differs radically from his second method in which all three sets of squinches are occupied at different levels, so that there are three, instead of two placements of layers. By this new means the N squinches are never used, since the placements alternate: S, S', S, S', etc., thus leaving vertical holes from bottom to top. This new, or third, method could have the second layer on the N squinches, instead of S', and then alternate S, N, S, N, leaving the S' squinches free; but in this particular case (Fig. 1), there would not be a vertical hole in the center.

Return to Question 2, page 85.

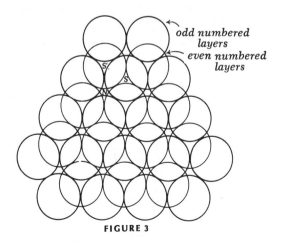

odd numbered
layers
even numbered
layers

FIGURE 3

The reason a hexagon is used instead of a triangle for the first layer is merely that the corners of the triangle would be superfluous; in any triangle, no matter how big, the squinch formed by the corner is always of the same type as the center one, where the flag is to go. That is, if we put a ball on the corner squinch, we find the center one will be occupied, and if we don't, the corner ball of the first layer is unnecessary, because it supports nothing. (The larger we make the hexagonal bottom layer, the more nearly regular it can be made.)

The way in which the three methods are related is as follows: The first and second are identical except that they are tilted from one another at 60°. When a sufficient amount has been piled in the triangular (second) way, we begin to see the same square pattern in layers that are at an angle with the bottom triangle (Fig. 4). The six balls in the square relationship are drawn solid, and the others dotted. The pairs AA, BB, and CC are in the bottom, second, and third layers respectively. Any set of balls taken at the same angle will be in the square arrangement.

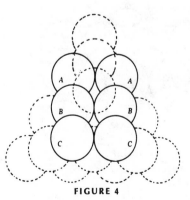

FIGURE 4

The best way to analyze the three methods is to consider the fact that in all three any ball is in contact with twelve others—excluding, of course, those on the outside—and we can continue these arrangements indefinitely in all directions. The centers of the twelve balls (with the thirteenth in the middle) form a fourteen-sided polyhedron (Fig. 5), in the first and second arrangements. In the third the polyhedron is similar, but the top half is twisted 60° (Fig. 6), bringing the top triangle into alignment with the base. Figure 7 shows how these polyhedra occur in the three arrangements.

Return to Question 2, page 85.

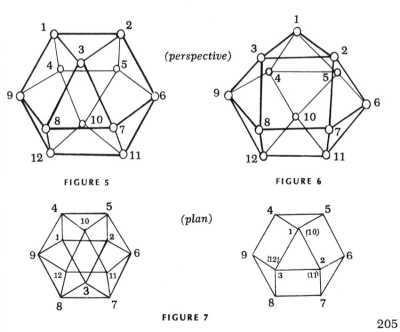

(perspective)

FIGURE 5

FIGURE 6

(plan)

FIGURE 7

Answer 2 *continued*

No; because method one starts with an indefinitely large square arrangement, and such a continuous plane of squares does not occur at any angle in the third method: the squares are in continuous rows, but the rows are staggered. Consequently we would have to build on a non-flat surface to accommodate these unevenly placed rows.

Figure 9 shows the plan of method three, starting next a corner with balls 1 and 5 in the first layer, and the two balls 2 and 6 in the second layer, which form a square with 1 and 5. The angle (α) of the plane of this square to the base is seen to be that of the edge, 1, 2, of the tetrahedron formed by the four balls 1, 2, 3, 4 ($\alpha = 55°$, almost). We consider only the balls on a line S-S to the right of 1. They, and the row above that form the squares, are shown solid; a few of the others are shown dotted. We now give, at a larger scale (Fig. 10), the view from the side—from the direction given by the arrow (Fig. 9)—of the balls in a vertical plane through S-S. The four to the left and above S-S would be there if the arrangement were made

FIGURE 9

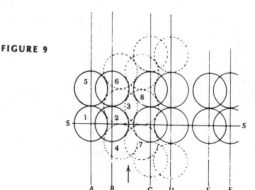

larger. They, all of them, occur only on the vertical lines marked *A, B, C, D, E, F,* etc. Two balls are shown dotted in placements *x* that occur only in other vertical planes, and cannot form squares with any balls in the given plane through *S-S.* The layers are numbered at the right.

We can now see that the rows of squares, of which only the ends are shown, e.g., 1, 2, are first on the slanting plane, *A-A',* for two layers, then for four layers they are not, then again on it for two layers, 7 and 8, etc. Consequently to make a pile with *A-A'* as the *horizontal* bottom layer, we should have to have a base with a stepped surface, and the patriot's flag would be at a sad angle—*α.*

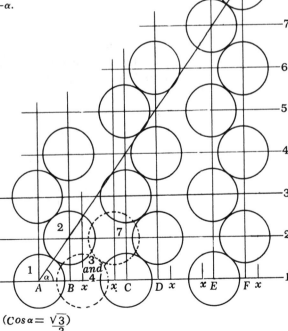

FIGURE 10

$$(Cos\,\alpha = \frac{\sqrt{3}}{3})$$

62

THE PILLAR OF CHIOS

They were the same.

Proof: We shall consider one of the four hemicylindrical covers, a, and one quarter of the square replacement pillar, ABC, and demonstrate their equality.

D is the midpoint of the side AC, and we make $x = 1$. Then $y = \sqrt{2}$.

$$\text{Area of } a = \frac{\pi}{2} - \left(\frac{\pi \sqrt{2}^2}{4} - \frac{\sqrt{2}^2}{2} \right)$$
$$= \frac{\pi}{2} - \frac{\pi \times 2}{4} + \frac{2}{2}$$
$$= 1$$
$$\text{Area of } ABC = \frac{\sqrt{2}^2}{2} = 1$$

Q.E.D.

The attentive, nondeaf goldsmith was a pupil of Hippocrates (not the doctor), who discovered the above ratio.

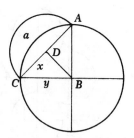

63

LITERARY QUIZ

Column 2 should read:

- (22) Abraham
- (11) Aeschylus
- (18) Aquinas
- (3) Aristophanes
- (6) Ascham
- (20) Athanasius
- (13) Boccaccio
- (5) Chaucer
- (2) Eusebius
- (15) Francis I
- (8) St. Gregory of Nyssa
- (17) Hippocrates
- (7) Homer
- (12) Herodotus
- (14) Miller (Joe)
- (23) Mississippi
- (9) Mohammed II
- (19) Palestrina
- (21) Rabelais
- (16) Satan
- (4) Tallis
- (10) Terpander
- (1) Walton

64

THUNDER ON THE RIGHT

Anywhere on a hyperbola, with focus at F.

The general definition of a hyperbola given in geometry books is: the locus of a point which moves so that the difference of its distances from two fixed points is constant. This is fulfilled by what is known to P of the source, S, i.e., wherever S is, it is 2 mi. nearer F than P.

The diagram shows the source at its nearest possible position, S', with $a = b - 2$; thus $b = a + 2$

$\therefore a + a + 2 = 4$, so $a = 1$ and $b = 3$

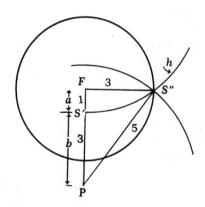

Due east.

We can ignore the hyperbola, h, and concentrate on the time elapsed between the flash and the sound reaching P not over the phone but from outside. The flash was reported by F as being calculably 15 sec. prior to his hearing the sound —at the same moment P heard it on the phone, and therefore 25 sec. before P heard it outside. Thus S was 5 mi. away from P. In the diagram the arc with center P has a radius of 5, and intersects the circle with center F and radius of 3, at S''. The triangle $S''PF$ has sides measuring 5, 4, and 3, and is therefore a right-angled triangle, and S'' is directly east of F.

65

TWO TRIANGLES

Total: 18 quadrilaterals (known so far).

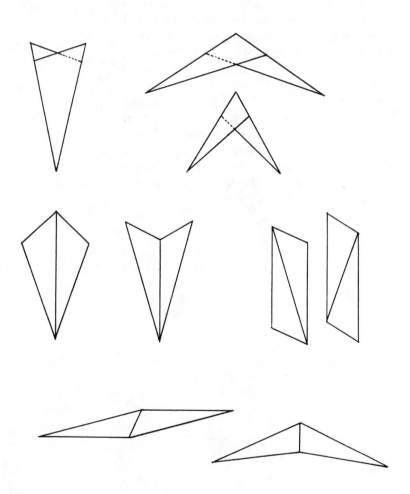

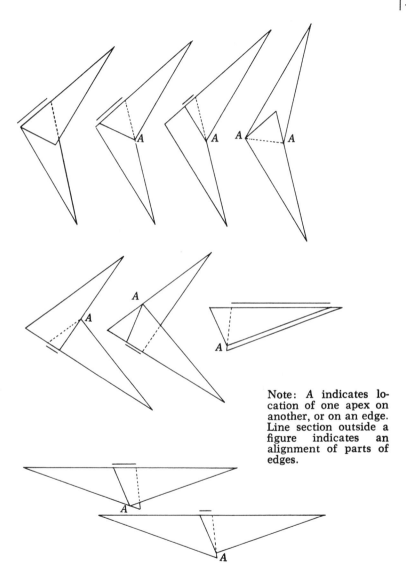

Note: *A* indicates location of one apex on another, or on an edge. Line section outside a figure indicates an alignment of parts of edges.

ANSWERS TO
SUBMISCELLANY

1   Wet ground glass. The clean cloth must be dry. The commonest example in a kitchen might be a Pyrex baking dish that had become worn or scratched on the bottom, so as to be merely translucent. When wet it is clear.

2   Queen Elizabeth. Freezing rain can make tiny 1-in. icicles on trees. Icicles more than 1 in. long rarely form in nature except at waterfalls, and she undoubtedly saw more houses than her American contemporary did waterfalls, and one waterfall usually keeps the same set of icicles all winter, whereas a heated house, especially in England, keeps melting them and forming new ones. Wigwams have no eaves. English houses were badly insulated; winters warmer. Algonquin women rarely hunted.

3   His right elbow is on his left knee.

4   Two parts Crème Yvette (violet), and one part Crème de Menthe (green), shaken up with beaten egg white (otherwise the blue is rather dark). The green cancels the red component of the violet, leaving blue. Not as nasty as it sounds, with a little lime.

5   An English accent. The English billion is 1,000,000,-000,000. He must have been referring to 999,999,000,001; if it were instead, 999,000,000,001, he would call it nine hundred and ninety-nine thousand million and one. In America the first number would be called nine hundred and ninety-nine billion, nine hundred and ninety-nine million and one.

6   Fire.

7   57. The trick is to take the things in order of complexity; start with dots, then lines, then circles, then squares, then letters. When you've reached 16 for the dots, keep on going with 17, etc., for the others.

8   According to size, not weight. Counting from the bottom up: cork fragments, barley, buckshot, marbles.

9   They overlap. Iceland (according to the National Geographic Society *et al.*) is in Europe, and its west coast is 200 mi. west of 17° west meridian, which runs through Shannon Island, the eastern outpost of Greenland (part of North America).

10   Up Fifth Avenue. It would take you through northern Europe, but east on Forty-second Street just misses South Africa, and doesn't hit land until Asia. To be seen, one must test it on a large globe with a great-circle ring (or wait for the Ice Age).

11   Shanghai. (Tokyo is biggest, London next, New York third.)

12   Almost none. It doesn't always work, but usually it all stays on the bottom until bumped or heated.

13   90.

14   Figure 1 shows the rain from a 100-mi. stretch of clouds falling at an angle of 45°; it wets the same extent of ground that it would if it fell vertically (but moved to the left), and to the same extent. The point is that the ground area is being compared with the cloud area, to which it is parallel, but in the case of the tilted roof (Fig. 1), it was not. Therefore, 100 mi. of cloud wet 100 mi. of ground; 10 in. of cloud wet 14 in. of roof.

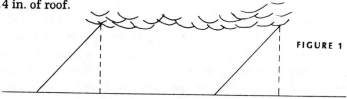

FIGURE 1

15   Uncooked rice, piled at an angle (Fig. 2). By shutting the windows and turning on the heat (it's freezing), and waiting. Figure 3 shows contents and arrangement.

218

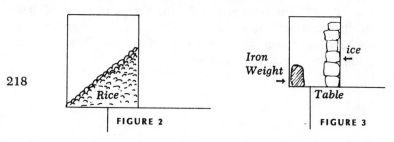

Rice

FIGURE 2

Iron Weight →

ice ←

Table

FIGURE 3

16   A hyperbola. If the reader remembers the definition of this curve in the answer to Puzzle 63, he will realize that the center, C, of the balloon will move so that its distance from the edge, E, will always equal the balloon's radius, and at any given position its distance from the center of the hemicylinder will always equal the radius of the balloon plus the radius of the cylindrical lid. This fulfills the definition.

17   Not *more* than 15 numbered pages. The clue is the page having an even number followed by an odd; manuscript pages are numbered odd on the front of each page, starting with 1 for the first, so a page (a side), or an odd number of pages, must have been erased, thus carrying the number forward. Since we are told that the "middle sheet" was 6/7, there could have been a maximum of 3 erased pages, and the corresponding number of unchanged sheets beyond the middle (Fig. 4) shows the arrangement. If both sides were erased, the sheet would be discarded.

FIGURE 4

$$\frac{1}{2} \quad \frac{2}{3} \quad \frac{3}{4} \quad \frac{4}{5} \quad \frac{6}{7} \quad \frac{8}{9} \quad \frac{10}{11} \quad \frac{12}{13} \quad \frac{14}{15}$$

18   Colorado and Wyoming are rectangles; Hawaii is an island.

19   Yes. Hold the handle and slide the pan back and forth about an inch so that the water begins to hump up in the middle; it is easy to find the right speed of oscillation; the water does not swing back and forth, but soon forms a peak, and throws up blobs which can be caught in the cup.

20   The shelf will be too short. When twenty volumes of this size are stacked on their sides, their weight will compress them so that there will be much too tight a fit to get them in and out of a shelf whose length is the height of the pile.

21   If one is wearing glasses, one pulls a sweater off by its neck, thereby stretching it open in front. Pulling it on has the reverse effect, and it catches on the glasses, for the neck gets tighter, if anything.

22   A. We are looking the eastern side of the Rock, with Spain to the right and the Mediterranean to the left.

23   Peter. The missing word—which was not asked for—is *Satan* (Matt. 16:23).

24   Matchbooks. They are arranged with their narrow ends alternating, so that the missing one leaves two pointing the same way.

25   Neither. It is totally impossible to fold it ten times. (Try it.)

26   A point, *P*, at the middle of the side, because most if not all oval dishes have rims of constant width. Figure 5 shows that the distance from rim to base, *B*, which acts as fulcrum, bears a greater proportion to the distance from *B* to center, *C*, when we press at *P* than if we press at *E*.

FIGURE 5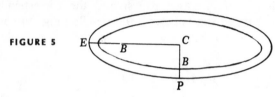

27   Three, if you're lucky, unless you thoroughly soap the inside of the bag. (Try it.)

28   Gravity. It makes it inconvenient to pile things up; thus most shelves have greater length than headroom. Thus variation in width matters less than having even one box or jar much higher than the rest. Refrigerators are crowded both ways.

29   Higher than the sun is from the earth. (Don't try it.)

30   About 4,500 mi. It involves the Bionomical Theorem: There are no wild penguins north of the Galapagos Islands, which are on the equator, and polar bears rarely swim more than 40 mi. from shore.

31   Yes; by stirring the water in the small bowl very fast.

32   6 = SIX becomes 9 = IX.

33   Lake of the Woods, Minnesota; it extends into Manitoba, Canada, over 25 mi. north of the 49th parallel. (The latter is over 100 mi. north of Maine.) There is some land, too.

34   TH. The pairs of consonants in STaNDaRDoaTH are the endings of the ordinal numbers, firST, secoND, thiRD, fourTH.

35   Go to the tree and pin a bit of white paper to it 6 ft. from the ground; go back to the house and put a pile of books on a table near a window that overlooks the pine. On the books put a bent piece of cardboard, over the top of which we can see the top and bottom of the pine and the bit of paper; mark off—or get someone to mark off—the position of these three points on the window, and measure them. The pine will almost certainly be very nearly vertical and thus parallel to the window. Simple proportion will give the required height.

36   One. King James VI of Scotland was crowned king of England as James I, in 1603. The others when crowned were all princes or dukes, etc.

37   $\sqrt{3} - \frac{\pi}{2}$ sq. ft.

Continue the pattern to form a rectangle; by Pythagoras, $h = \sqrt{3}$. By symmetry the area of the new dark part, A, equals the area of B. The area of $A + C$ equals the area of the rectangle minus half the area of a circle with radius 1, or $\sqrt{3} - \frac{\pi}{2}$.

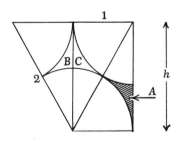

38 Work.

39 The sun and a lamp, when "out."

40 None. You will be more than 20 mi. *east* of it.

41 The medicine closet probably contains a transparent cylindrical plastic pillbox; empty it and hold the cigarette pinched between the base of two fingers, so that the lit end projects no more than half the length of the box, and put it inside (see Fig. 6), pressing the two fingers tightly against the circular opening to exclude air. The carbon dioxide puts the fire out very fast.

Push

FIGURE 6

42 Semisopochnoi Island, in the Aleutians. Not Quoddy Head, Maine, the longitude of which is just less than 67°W. The Aleutians cross the 180th meridian, and Semisopochnoi (the Russian name is suggestive of its position) is at longitude 179°40′ E., approximately.

43 10. Some people forget to include Y; still others include *U* which has a Y sound, but so has "unit." The following list gives all the initials of the spoken alphabet:

A B C D E E G A I J K E E E O P Q A E T U V D E W Z

44 Oh my chronology's askew! (Omicron -ology's askew)

45 *Punta Marroqui:* a few miles south of Gibraltar. *Cape Agulhas:* over 30 mi. south of Cape of Good Hope. *Diego Ramirez Islands:* about 45 mi. south of Cape Horn. It is not on the mainland, but neither is the Cape.

46 Rack railway. The pinion supports the engine in that it prevents it from running downhill.

47 Two teaspoonfuls. Call the amount that sticks to the inside of the spoon, x: we have to assume that x also sticks to the under side, otherwise the problem cannot be solved, and anyway it has nearly the same area. Therefore, calling the dry spoonful 1, if 1 wet spoonful is put into the cup *with* the spoon, $1 + x$ is delivered: with 2 it would be $1 - x$ and $1 + x$, or 2: with 3 it would be $1 - x + 1 - x + 1 + x$, or $3 - x$: with 4 it would be $4 - 2x$. The expression is, if $n =$ number of spoonings, the delivered amount is $n(1 - x) + x$, which is asymptotic to $n(1 - x)$. In other words he wanted, and got, two.

48 Airmail is figured by fractions of ounces. He gave his letters unstamped to be weighed by the clerk, who then sold him the right stamps to be put on afterward. Their weight could frequently have made just enough difference to require more postage.

49 Mercury and water. The former can be got from a thermometer by breaking. The water stays on top and can be poured off, and any traces removed with blotting paper or just waiting. Oils leave a nearly unremovable film on both water and mercury.

50 "I do."

ENVOI

(with apologies to John Lyly)

Euclid and my Arachne played
At Geometrics,
Euclid prayed.
Arachne raised him—in the pot
She threw her spindle.
"That's the lot,"
She cried, and Euclid, nothing loath,
Bet pen and compass,
Losing both.
Then he put up his dearest prize;
The Golden Section,
But his eyes
Narrow. "If I'm not being trite
"The angles of a square
"Are right."
She says, "But of this tetragon,
"Whose angles, each
"And every one,
"Are *more* than right, what do you say?"
Poor Euclid now
Has turned away,
And mumbles as his spirits ebb,
"It isn't *fair*,
"It's made of web!"

A CATALOG OF SELECTED
DOVER BOOKS
IN ALL FIELDS OF INTEREST

A CATALOG OF SELECTED DOVER BOOKS IN ALL FIELDS OF INTEREST

DRAWINGS OF REMBRANDT, edited by Seymour Slive. Updated Lippmann, Hofstede de Groot edition, with definitive scholarly apparatus. All portraits, biblical sketches, landscapes, nudes. Oriental figures, classical studies, together with selection of work by followers. 550 illustrations. Total of 630pp. 9⅛ × 12¼.
21485-0, 21486-9 Pa., Two-vol. set $25.00

GHOST AND HORROR STORIES OF AMBROSE BIERCE, Ambrose Bierce. 24 tales vividly imagined, strangely prophetic, and decades ahead of their time in technical skill: "The Damned Thing," "An Inhabitant of Carcosa," "The Eyes of the Panther," "Moxon's Master," and 20 more. 199pp. 5⅜ × 8½. 20767-6 Pa. $3.95

ETHICAL WRITINGS OF MAIMONIDES, Maimonides. Most significant ethical works of great medieval sage, newly translated for utmost precision, readability. Laws Concerning Character Traits, Eight Chapters, more. 192pp. 5⅜ × 8½.
24522-5 Pa. $4.50

THE EXPLORATION OF THE COLORADO RIVER AND ITS CANYONS, J. W. Powell. Full text of Powell's 1,000-mile expedition down the fabled Colorado in 1869. Superb account of terrain, geology, vegetation, Indians, famine, mutiny, treacherous rapids, mighty canyons, during exploration of last unknown part of continental U.S. 400pp. 5⅜ × 8½. 20094-9 Pa. $6.95

HISTORY OF PHILOSOPHY, Julián Marías. Clearest one-volume history on the market. Every major philosopher and dozens of others, to Existentialism and later. 505pp. 5⅜ × 8½. 21739-6 Pa. $8.50

ALL ABOUT LIGHTNING, Martin A. Uman. Highly readable non-technical survey of nature and causes of lightning, thunderstorms, ball lightning, St. Elmo's Fire, much more. Illustrated. 192pp. 5⅜ × 8½. 25237-X Pa. $5.95

SAILING ALONE AROUND THE WORLD, Captain Joshua Slocum. First man to sail around the world, alone, in small boat. One of great feats of seamanship told in delightful manner. 67 illustrations. 294pp. 5⅜ × 8½. 20326-3 Pa. $4.95

LETTERS AND NOTES ON THE MANNERS, CUSTOMS AND CONDITIONS OF THE NORTH AMERICAN INDIANS, George Catlin. Classic account of life among Plains Indians: ceremonies, hunt, warfare, etc. 312 plates. 572pp. of text. 6⅛ × 9¼. 22118-0, 22119-9 Pa. Two-vol. set $15.90

ALASKA: The Harriman Expedition, 1899, John Burroughs, John Muir, et al. Informative, engrossing accounts of two-month, 9,000-mile expedition. Native peoples, wildlife, forests, geography, salmon industry, glaciers, more. Profusely illustrated. 240 black-and-white line drawings. 124 black-and-white photographs. 3 maps. Index. 576pp. 5⅜ × 8½. 25109-8 Pa. $11.95

THE BOOK OF BEASTS: Being a Translation from a Latin Bestiary of the Twelfth Century, T. H. White. Wonderful catalog real and fanciful beasts: manticore, griffin, phoenix, amphivius, jaculus, many more. White's witty erudite commentary on scientific, historical aspects. Fascinating glimpse of medieval mind. Illustrated. 296pp. 5⅜ × 8¼. (Available in U.S. only) 24609-4 Pa. $5.95

FRANK LLOYD WRIGHT: ARCHITECTURE AND NATURE With 160 Illustrations, Donald Hoffmann. Profusely illustrated study of influence of nature—especially prairie—on Wright's designs for Fallingwater, Robie House, Guggenheim Museum, other masterpieces. 96pp. 9¼ × 10¾. 25098-9 Pa. $7.95

FRANK LLOYD WRIGHT'S FALLINGWATER, Donald Hoffmann. Wright's famous waterfall house: planning and construction of organic idea. History of site, owners, Wright's personal involvement. Photographs of various stages of building. Preface by Edgar Kaufmann, Jr. 100 illustrations. 112pp. 9¼ × 10.
23671-4 Pa. $7.95

YEARS WITH FRANK LLOYD WRIGHT: Apprentice to Genius, Edgar Tafel. Insightful memoir by a former apprentice presents a revealing portrait of Wright the man, the inspired teacher, the greatest American architect. 372 black-and-white illustrations. Preface. Index. vi + 228pp. 8¼ × 11. 24801-1 Pa. $9.95

THE STORY OF KING ARTHUR AND HIS KNIGHTS, Howard Pyle. Enchanting version of King Arthur fable has delighted generations with imaginative narratives of exciting adventures and unforgettable illustrations by the author. 41 illustrations. xviii + 313pp. 6⅛ × 9¼. 21445-1 Pa. $6.50

THE GODS OF THE EGYPTIANS, E. A. Wallis Budge. Thorough coverage of numerous gods of ancient Egypt by foremost Egyptologist. Information on evolution of cults, rites and gods; the cult of Osiris; the Book of the Dead and its rites; the sacred animals and birds; Heaven and Hell; and more. 956pp. 6⅛ × 9¼.
22055-9, 22056-7 Pa., Two-vol. set $20.00

A THEOLOGICO-POLITICAL TREATISE, Benedict Spinoza. Also contains unfinished *Political Treatise*. Great classic on religious liberty, theory of government on common consent. R. Elwes translation. Total of 421pp. 5⅜ × 8½.
20249-6 Pa. $6.95

INCIDENTS OF TRAVEL IN CENTRAL AMERICA, CHIAPAS, AND YUCATAN, John L. Stephens. Almost single-handed discovery of Maya culture; exploration of ruined cities, monuments, temples; customs of Indians. 115 drawings. 892pp. 5⅜ × 8½. 22404-X, 22405-8 Pa., Two-vol. set $15.90

LOS CAPRICHOS, Francisco Goya. 80 plates of wild, grotesque monsters and caricatures. Prado manuscript included. 183pp. 6⅜ × 9⅝. 22384-1 Pa. $4.95

AUTOBIOGRAPHY: The Story of My Experiments with Truth, Mohandas K. Gandhi. Not hagiography, but Gandhi in his own words. Boyhood, legal studies, purification, the growth of the Satyagraha (nonviolent protest) movement. Critical, inspiring work of the man who freed India. 480pp. 5⅜ × 8½. (Available in U.S. only)
24593-4 Pa. $6.95

ILLUSTRATED DICTIONARY OF HISTORIC ARCHITECTURE, edited by Cyril M. Harris. Extraordinary compendium of clear, concise definitions for over 5,000 important architectural terms complemented by over 2,000 line drawings. Covers full spectrum of architecture from ancient ruins to 20th-century Modernism. Preface. 592pp. 7½ × 9⅜. 24444-X Pa. $14.95

THE NIGHT BEFORE CHRISTMAS, Clement Moore. Full text, and woodcuts from original 1848 book. Also critical, historical material. 19 illustrations. 40pp. 4⅝ × 6. 22797-9 Pa. $2.25

THE LESSON OF JAPANESE ARCHITECTURE: 165 Photographs, Jiro Harada. Memorable gallery of 165 photographs taken in the 1930's of exquisite Japanese homes of the well-to-do and historic buildings. 13 line diagrams. 192pp. 8⅜ × 11¼. 24778-3 Pa. $8.95

THE AUTOBIOGRAPHY OF CHARLES DARWIN AND SELECTED LETTERS, edited by Francis Darwin. The fascinating life of eccentric genius composed of an intimate memoir by Darwin (intended for his children); commentary by his son, Francis; hundreds of fragments from notebooks, journals, papers; and letters to and from Lyell, Hooker, Huxley, Wallace and Henslow. xi + 365pp. 5⅜ × 8. 20479-0 Pa. $6.95

WONDERS OF THE SKY: Observing Rainbows, Comets, Eclipses, the Stars and Other Phenomena, Fred Schaaf. Charming, easy-to-read poetic guide to all manner of celestial events visible to the naked eye. Mock suns, glories, Belt of Venus, more. Illustrated. 299pp. 5¼ × 8¼. 24402-4 Pa. $7.95

BURNHAM'S CELESTIAL HANDBOOK, Robert Burnham, Jr. Thorough guide to the stars beyond our solar system. Exhaustive treatment. Alphabetical by constellation: Andromeda to Cetus in Vol. 1; Chamaeleon to Orion in Vol. 2; and Pavo to Vulpecula in Vol. 3. Hundreds of illustrations. Index in Vol. 3. 2,000pp. 6⅛ × 9¼. 23567-X, 23568-8, 23673-0 Pa., Three-vol. set $38.85

STAR NAMES: Their Lore and Meaning, Richard Hinckley Allen. Fascinating history of names various cultures have given to constellations and literary and folkloristic uses that have been made of stars. Indexes to subjects. Arabic and Greek names. Biblical references. Bibliography. 563pp. 5⅜ × 8½. 21079-0 Pa. $7.95

THIRTY YEARS THAT SHOOK PHYSICS: The Story of Quantum Theory, George Gamow. Lucid, accessible introduction to influential theory of energy and matter. Careful explanations of Dirac's anti-particles, Bohr's model of the atom, much more. 12 plates. Numerous drawings. 240pp. 5⅜ × 8½. 24895-X Pa. $4.95

CHINESE DOMESTIC FURNITURE IN PHOTOGRAPHS AND MEASURED DRAWINGS, Gustav Ecke. A rare volume, now affordably priced for antique collectors, furniture buffs and art historians. Detailed review of styles ranging from early Shang to late Ming. Unabridged republication. 161 black-and-white drawings, photos. Total of 224pp. 8⅜ × 11¼. (Available in U.S. only) 25171-3 Pa. $12.95

VINCENT VAN GOGH: A Biography, Julius Meier-Graefe. Dynamic, penetrating study of artist's life, relationship with brother, Theo, painting techniques, travels, more. Readable, engrossing. 160pp. 5⅜ × 8½. (Available in U.S. only) 25253-1 Pa. $3.95

HOW TO WRITE, Gertrude Stein. Gertrude Stein claimed anyone could understand her unconventional writing—here are clues to help. Fascinating improvisations, language experiments, explanations illuminate Stein's craft and the art of writing. Total of 414pp. 4⅝ × 6⅜. 23144-5 Pa. $5.95

ADVENTURES AT SEA IN THE GREAT AGE OF SAIL: Five Firsthand Narratives, edited by Elliot Snow. Rare true accounts of exploration, whaling, shipwreck, fierce natives, trade, shipboard life, more. 33 illustrations. Introduction. 353pp. 5⅜ × 8½. 25177-2 Pa. $7.95

THE HERBAL OR GENERAL HISTORY OF PLANTS, John Gerard. Classic descriptions of about 2,850 plants—with over 2,700 illustrations—includes Latin and English names, physical descriptions, varieties, time and place of growth, more. 2,706 illustrations. xlv + 1,678pp. 8½ × 12¼. 23147-X Cloth. $75.00

DOROTHY AND THE WIZARD IN OZ, L. Frank Baum. Dorothy and the Wizard visit the center of the Earth, where people are vegetables, glass houses grow and Oz characters reappear. Classic sequel to *Wizard of Oz*. 256pp. 5⅜ × 8.
24714-7 Pa. $4.95

SONGS OF EXPERIENCE: Facsimile Reproduction with 26 Plates in Full Color, William Blake. This facsimile of Blake's original "Illuminated Book" reproduces 26 full-color plates from a rare 1826 edition. Includes "The Tyger," "London," "Holy Thursday," and other immortal poems. 26 color plates. Printed text of poems. 48pp. 5¼ × 7. 24636-1 Pa. $3.50

SONGS OF INNOCENCE, William Blake. The first and most popular of Blake's famous "Illuminated Books," in a facsimile edition reproducing all 31 brightly colored plates. Additional printed text of each poem. 64pp. 5¼ × 7.
22764-2 Pa. $3.50

PRECIOUS STONES, Max Bauer. Classic, thorough study of diamonds, rubies, emeralds, garnets, etc.: physical character, occurrence, properties, use, similar topics. 20 plates, 8 in color. 94 figures. 659pp. 6⅛ × 9¼.
21910-0, 21911-9 Pa., Two-vol. set $15.90

ENCYCLOPEDIA OF VICTORIAN NEEDLEWORK, S. F. A. Caulfeild and Blanche Saward. Full, precise descriptions of stitches, techniques for dozens of needlecrafts—most exhaustive reference of its kind. Over 800 figures. Total of 679pp. 8¼ × 11. Two volumes. Vol. 1 22800-2 Pa. $11.95
Vol. 2 22801-0 Pa. $11.95

THE MARVELOUS LAND OF OZ, L. Frank Baum. Second Oz book, the Scarecrow and Tin Woodman are back with hero named Tip, Oz magic. 136 illustrations. 287pp. 5⅜ × 8½. 20692-0 Pa. $5.95

WILD FOWL DECOYS, Joel Barber. Basic book on the subject, by foremost authority and collector. Reveals history of decoy making and rigging, place in American culture, different kinds of decoys, how to make them, and how to use them. 140 plates. 156pp. 7⅞ × 10¾. 20011-6 Pa. $8.95

HISTORY OF LACE, Mrs. Bury Palliser. Definitive, profusely illustrated chronicle of lace from earliest times to late 19th century. Laces of Italy, Greece, England, France, Belgium, etc. Landmark of needlework scholarship. 266 illustrations. 672pp. 6⅛ × 9¼. 24742-2 Pa. $14.95

ILLUSTRATED GUIDE TO SHAKER FURNITURE, Robert Meader. All furniture and appurtenances, with much on unknown local styles. 235 photos. 146pp. 9 × 12. 22819-3 Pa. $7.95

WHALE SHIPS AND WHALING: A Pictorial Survey, George Francis Dow. Over 200 vintage engravings, drawings, photographs of barks, brigs, cutters, other vessels. Also harpoons, lances, whaling guns, many other artifacts. Comprehensive text by foremost authority. 207 black-and-white illustrations. 288pp. 6 × 9. 24808-9 Pa. $8.95

THE BERTRAMS, Anthony Trollope. Powerful portrayal of blind self-will and thwarted ambition includes one of Trollope's most heartrending love stories. 497pp. 5⅜ × 8½. 25119-5 Pa. $8.95

ADVENTURES WITH A HAND LENS, Richard Headstrom. Clearly written guide to observing and studying flowers and grasses, fish scales, moth and insect wings, egg cases, buds, feathers, seeds, leaf scars, moss, molds, ferns, common crystals, etc.—all with an ordinary, inexpensive magnifying glass. 209 exact line drawings aid in your discoveries. 220pp. 5⅜ × 8½. 23330-8 Pa. $3.95

RODIN ON ART AND ARTISTS, Auguste Rodin. Great sculptor's candid, wide-ranging comments on meaning of art; great artists; relation of sculpture to poetry, painting, music; philosophy of life, more. 76 superb black-and-white illustrations of Rodin's sculpture, drawings and prints. 119pp. 8⅜ × 11¼. 24487-3 Pa. $6.95

FIFTY CLASSIC FRENCH FILMS, 1912–1982: A Pictorial Record, Anthony Slide. Memorable stills from Grand Illusion, Beauty and the Beast, Hiroshima, Mon Amour, many more. Credits, plot synopses, reviews, etc. 160pp. 8¼ × 11. 25256-6 Pa. $11.95

THE PRINCIPLES OF PSYCHOLOGY, William James. Famous long course complete, unabridged. Stream of thought, time perception, memory, experimental methods; great work decades ahead of its time. 94 figures. 1,391pp. 5⅜ × 8½. 20381-6, 20382-4 Pa., Two-vol. set $19.90

BODIES IN A BOOKSHOP, R. T. Campbell. Challenging mystery of blackmail and murder with ingenious plot and superbly drawn characters. In the best tradition of British suspense fiction. 192pp. 5⅜ × 8½. 24720-1 Pa. $3.95

CALLAS: PORTRAIT OF A PRIMA DONNA, George Jellinek. Renowned commentator on the musical scene chronicles incredible career and life of the most controversial, fascinating, influential operatic personality of our time. 64 black-and-white photographs. 416pp. 5⅜ × 8¼. 25047-4 Pa. $7.95

GEOMETRY, RELATIVITY AND THE FOURTH DIMENSION, Rudolph Rucker. Exposition of fourth dimension, concepts of relativity as Flatland characters continue adventures. Popular, easily followed yet accurate, profound. 141 illustrations. 133pp. 5⅜ × 8½. 23400-2 Pa. $3.95

HOUSEHOLD STORIES BY THE BROTHERS GRIMM, with pictures by Walter Crane. 53 classic stories—Rumpelstiltskin, Rapunzel, Hansel and Gretel, the Fisherman and his Wife, Snow White, Tom Thumb, Sleeping Beauty, Cinderella, and so much more—lavishly illustrated with original 19th century drawings. 114 illustrations. x + 269pp. 5⅜ × 8½. 21080-4 Pa. $4.50

SUNDIALS, Albert Waugh. Far and away the best, most thorough coverage of ideas, mathematics concerned, types, construction, adjusting anywhere. Over 100 illustrations. 230pp. 5⅜ × 8½. 22947-5 Pa. $4.50

PICTURE HISTORY OF THE NORMANDIE: With 190 Illustrations, Frank O. Braynard. Full story of legendary French ocean liner: Art Deco interiors, design innovations, furnishings, celebrities, maiden voyage, tragic fire, much more. Extensive text. 144pp. 8⅜ × 11¾. 25257-4 Pa. $9.95

THE FIRST AMERICAN COOKBOOK: A Facsimile of "American Cookery," 1796, Amelia Simmons. Facsimile of the first American-written cookbook published in the United States contains authentic recipes for colonial favorites—pumpkin pudding, winter squash pudding, spruce beer, Indian slapjacks, and more. Introductory Essay and Glossary of colonial cooking terms. 80pp. 5⅜ × 8½. 24710-4 Pa. $3.50

101 PUZZLES IN THOUGHT AND LOGIC, C. R. Wylie, Jr. Solve murders and robberies, find out which fishermen are liars, how a blind man could possibly identify a color—purely by your own reasoning! 107pp. 5⅜ × 8½. 20367-0 Pa. $2.50

THE BOOK OF WORLD-FAMOUS MUSIC—CLASSICAL, POPULAR AND FOLK, James J. Fuld. Revised and enlarged republication of landmark work in musico-bibliography. Full information about nearly 1,000 songs and compositions including first lines of music and lyrics. New supplement. Index. 800pp. 5⅜ × 8¼. 24857-7 Pa. $14.95

ANTHROPOLOGY AND MODERN LIFE, Franz Boas. Great anthropologist's classic treatise on race and culture. Introduction by Ruth Bunzel. Only inexpensive paperback edition. 255pp. 5⅜ × 8½. 25245-0 Pa. $5.95

THE TALE OF PETER RABBIT, Beatrix Potter. The inimitable Peter's terrifying adventure in Mr. McGregor's garden, with all 27 wonderful, full-color Potter illustrations. 55pp. 4¼ × 5½. (Available in U.S. only) 22827-4 Pa. $1.75

THREE PROPHETIC SCIENCE FICTION NOVELS, H. G. Wells. *When the Sleeper Wakes, A Story of the Days to Come* and *The Time Machine* (full version). 335pp. 5⅜ × 8½. (Available in U.S. only) 20605-X Pa. $5.95

APICIUS COOKERY AND DINING IN IMPERIAL ROME, edited and translated by Joseph Dommers Vehling. Oldest known cookbook in existence offers readers a clear picture of what foods Romans ate, how they prepared them, etc. 49 illustrations. 301pp. 6⅛ × 9¼. 23563-7 Pa. $6.50

SHAKESPEARE LEXICON AND QUOTATION DICTIONARY, Alexander Schmidt. Full definitions, locations, shades of meaning of every word in plays and poems. More than 50,000 exact quotations. 1,485pp. 6½ × 9¼. 22726-X, 22727-8 Pa., Two-vol. set $27.90

THE WORLD'S GREAT SPEECHES, edited by Lewis Copeland and Lawrence W. Lamm. Vast collection of 278 speeches from Greeks to 1970. Powerful and effective models; unique look at history. 842pp. 5⅜ × 8½. 20468-5 Pa. $11.95

THE BLUE FAIRY BOOK, Andrew Lang. The first, most famous collection, with many familiar tales: Little Red Riding Hood, Aladdin and the Wonderful Lamp, Puss in Boots, Sleeping Beauty, Hansel and Gretel, Rumpelstiltskin; 37 in all. 138 illustrations. 390pp. 5⅜ × 8½. 21437-0 Pa. $5.95

THE STORY OF THE CHAMPIONS OF THE ROUND TABLE, Howard Pyle. Sir Launcelot, Sir Tristram and Sir Percival in spirited adventures of love and triumph retold in Pyle's inimitable style. 50 drawings, 31 full-page. xviii + 329pp. 6½ × 9¼. 21883-X Pa. $6.95

AUDUBON AND HIS JOURNALS, Maria Audubon. Unmatched two-volume portrait of the great artist, naturalist and author contains his journals, an excellent biography by his granddaughter, expert annotations by the noted ornithologist, Dr. Elliott Coues, and 37 superb illustrations. Total of 1,200pp. 5⅜ × 8.
Vol. I 25143-8 Pa. $8.95
Vol. II 25144-6 Pa. $8.95

GREAT DINOSAUR HUNTERS AND THEIR DISCOVERIES, Edwin H. Colbert. Fascinating, lavishly illustrated chronicle of dinosaur research, 1820's to 1960. Achievements of Cope, Marsh, Brown, Buckland, Mantell, Huxley, many others. 384pp. 5¼ × 8¼. 24701-5 Pa. $6.95

THE TASTEMAKERS, Russell Lynes. Informal, illustrated social history of American taste 1850's–1950's. First popularized categories Highbrow, Lowbrow, Middlebrow. 129 illustrations. New (1979) afterword. 384pp. 6 × 9.
23993-4 Pa. $6.95

DOUBLE CROSS PURPOSES, Ronald A. Knox. A treasure hunt in the Scottish Highlands, an old map, unidentified corpse, surprise discoveries keep reader guessing in this cleverly intricate tale of financial skullduggery. 2 black-and-white maps. 320pp. 5⅜ × 8½. (Available in U.S. only) 25032-6 Pa. $5.95

AUTHENTIC VICTORIAN DECORATION AND ORNAMENTATION IN FULL COLOR: 46 Plates from "Studies in Design," Christopher Dresser. Superb full-color lithographs reproduced from rare original portfolio of a major Victorian designer. 48pp. 9¼ × 12¼. 25083-0 Pa. $7.95

PRIMITIVE ART, Franz Boas. Remains the best text ever prepared on subject, thoroughly discussing Indian, African, Asian, Australian, and, especially, Northern American primitive art. Over 950 illustrations show ceramics, masks, totem poles, weapons, textiles, paintings, much more. 376pp. 5⅜ × 8. 20025-6 Pa. $6.95

SIDELIGHTS ON RELATIVITY, Albert Einstein. Unabridged republication of two lectures delivered by the great physicist in 1920–21. *Ether and Relativity* and *Geometry and Experience*. Elegant ideas in non-mathematical form, accessible to intelligent layman. vi + 56pp. 5⅜ × 8½. 24511-X Pa. $2.95

THE WIT AND HUMOR OF OSCAR WILDE, edited by Alvin Redman. More than 1,000 ripostes, paradoxes, wisecracks: Work is the curse of the drinking classes, I can resist everything except temptation, etc. 258pp. 5⅜ × 8½. 20602-5 Pa. $4.50

ADVENTURES WITH A MICROSCOPE, Richard Headstrom. 59 adventures with clothing fibers, protozoa, ferns and lichens, roots and leaves, much more. 142 illustrations. 232pp. 5⅜ × 8½. 23471-1 Pa. $3.95

PLANTS OF THE BIBLE, Harold N. Moldenke and Alma L. Moldenke. Standard reference to all 230 plants mentioned in Scriptures. Latin name, biblical reference, uses, modern identity, much more. Unsurpassed encyclopedic resource for scholars, botanists, nature lovers, students of Bible. Bibliography. Indexes. 123 black-and-white illustrations. 384pp. 6 × 9. 25069-5 Pa. $8.95

FAMOUS AMERICAN WOMEN: A Biographical Dictionary from Colonial Times to the Present, Robert McHenry, ed. From Pocahontas to Rosa Parks, 1,035 distinguished American women documented in separate biographical entries. Accurate, up-to-date data, numerous categories, spans 400 years. Indices. 493pp. 6½ × 9¼. 24523-3 Pa. $9.95

THE FABULOUS INTERIORS OF THE GREAT OCEAN LINERS IN HISTORIC PHOTOGRAPHS, William H. Miller, Jr. Some 200 superb photographs capture exquisite interiors of world's great "floating palaces"—1890's to 1980's: *Titanic, Ile de France, Queen Elizabeth, United States, Europa,* more. Approx. 200 black-and-white photographs. Captions. Text. Introduction. 160pp. 8⅞ × 11¾. 24756-2 Pa. $9.95

THE GREAT LUXURY LINERS, 1927–1954: A Photographic Record, William H. Miller, Jr. Nostalgic tribute to heyday of ocean liners. 186 photos of Ile de France, Normandie, Leviathan, Queen Elizabeth, United States, many others. Interior and exterior views. Introduction. Captions. 160pp. 9 × 12. 24056-8 Pa. $9.95

A NATURAL HISTORY OF THE DUCKS, John Charles Phillips. Great landmark of ornithology offers complete detailed coverage of nearly 200 species and subspecies of ducks: gadwall, sheldrake, merganser, pintail, many more. 74 full-color plates, 102 black-and-white. Bibliography. Total of 1,920pp. 8⅝ × 11¼. 25141-1, 25142-X Cloth. Two-vol. set $100.00

THE SEAWEED HANDBOOK: An Illustrated Guide to Seaweeds from North Carolina to Canada, Thomas F. Lee. Concise reference covers 78 species. Scientific and common names, habitat, distribution, more. Finding keys for easy identification. 224pp. 5⅜ × 8½. 25215-9 Pa. $5.95

THE TEN BOOKS OF ARCHITECTURE: The 1755 Leoni Edition, Leon Battista Alberti. Rare classic helped introduce the glories of ancient architecture to the Renaissance. 68 black-and-white plates. 336pp. 8⅜ × 11¼. 25239-6 Pa. $14.95

MISS MACKENZIE, Anthony Trollope. Minor masterpieces by Victorian master unmasks many truths about life in 19th-century England. First inexpensive edition in years. 392pp. 5⅜ × 8½. 25201-9 Pa. $7.95

THE RIME OF THE ANCIENT MARINER, Gustave Doré, Samuel Taylor Coleridge. Dramatic engravings considered by many to be his greatest work. The terrifying space of the open sea, the storms and whirlpools of an unknown ocean, the ice of Antarctica, more—all rendered in a powerful, chilling manner. Full text. 38 plates. 77pp. 9¼ × 12. 22305-1 Pa. $4.95

THE EXPEDITIONS OF ZEBULON MONTGOMERY PIKE, Zebulon Montgomery Pike. Fascinating first-hand accounts (1805–6) of exploration of Mississippi River, Indian wars, capture by Spanish dragoons, much more. 1,088pp. 5⅜ × 8½. 25254-X, 25255-8 Pa. Two-vol. set $23.90

A CONCISE HISTORY OF PHOTOGRAPHY: Third Revised Edition, Helmut Gernsheim. Best one-volume history—camera obscura, photochemistry, daguerreotypes, evolution of cameras, film, more. Also artistic aspects—landscape, portraits, fine art, etc. 281 black-and-white photographs. 26 in color. 176pp. 8⅜ × 11¼. 25128-4 Pa. $12.95

THE DORÉ BIBLE ILLUSTRATIONS, Gustave Doré. 241 detailed plates from the Bible: the Creation scenes, Adam and Eve, Flood, Babylon, battle sequences, life of Jesus, etc. Each plate is accompanied by the verses from the King James version of the Bible. 241pp. 9 × 12. 23004-X Pa. $8.95

HUGGER-MUGGER IN THE LOUVRE, Elliot Paul. Second Homer Evans mystery-comedy. Theft at the Louvre involves sleuth in hilarious, madcap caper. "A knockout."—Books. 336pp. 5⅜ × 8½. 25185-3 Pa. $5.95

FLATLAND, E. A. Abbott. Intriguing and enormously popular science-fiction classic explores the complexities of trying to survive as a two-dimensional being in a three-dimensional world. Amusingly illustrated by the author. 16 illustrations. 103pp. 5⅜ × 8½. 20001-9 Pa. $2.25

THE HISTORY OF THE LEWIS AND CLARK EXPEDITION, Meriwether Lewis and William Clark, edited by Elliott Coues. Classic edition of Lewis and Clark's day-by-day journals that later became the basis for U.S. claims to Oregon and the West. Accurate and invaluable geographical, botanical, biological, meteorological and anthropological material. Total of 1,508pp. 5⅜ × 8½.
21268-8, 21269-6, 21270-X Pa. Three-vol. set $25.50

LANGUAGE, TRUTH AND LOGIC, Alfred J. Ayer. Famous, clear introduction to Vienna, Cambridge schools of Logical Positivism. Role of philosophy, elimination of metaphysics, nature of analysis, etc. 160pp. 5⅜ × 8½. (Available in U.S. and Canada only) 20010-8 Pa. $2.95

MATHEMATICS FOR THE NONMATHEMATICIAN, Morris Kline. Detailed, college-level treatment of mathematics in cultural and historical context, with numerous exercises. For liberal arts students. Preface. Recommended Reading Lists. Tables. Index. Numerous black-and-white figures. xvi + 641pp. 5⅜ × 8½.
24823-2 Pa. $11.95

28 SCIENCE FICTION STORIES, H. G. Wells. Novels, *Star Begotten* and *Men Like Gods,* plus 26 short stories: "Empire of the Ants," "A Story of the Stone Age," "The Stolen Bacillus," "In the Abyss," etc. 915pp. 5⅜ × 8½. (Available in U.S. only)
20265-8 Cloth. $10.95

HANDBOOK OF PICTORIAL SYMBOLS, Rudolph Modley. 3,250 signs and symbols, many systems in full; official or heavy commercial use. Arranged by subject. Most in Pictorial Archive series. 143pp. 8⅛ × 11. 23357-X Pa. $5.95

INCIDENTS OF TRAVEL IN YUCATAN, John L. Stephens. Classic (1843) exploration of jungles of Yucatan, looking for evidences of Maya civilization. Travel adventures, Mexican and Indian culture, etc. Total of 669pp. 5⅜ × 8½.
20926-1, 20927-X Pa., Two-vol. set $9.90

DEGAS: An Intimate Portrait, Ambroise Vollard. Charming, anecdotal memoir by famous art dealer of one of the greatest 19th-century French painters. 14 black-and-white illustrations. Introduction by Harold L. Van Doren. 96pp. 5⅜ × 8½.
25131-4 Pa. $3.95

PERSONAL NARRATIVE OF A PILGRIMAGE TO ALMANDINAH AND MECCAH, Richard Burton. Great travel classic by remarkably colorful personality. Burton, disguised as a Moroccan, visited sacred shrines of Islam, narrowly escaping death. 47 illustrations. 959pp. 5⅜ × 8½. 21217-3, 21218-1 Pa., Two-vol. set $19.90

PHRASE AND WORD ORIGINS, A. H. Holt. Entertaining, reliable, modern study of more than 1,200 colorful words, phrases, origins and histories. Much unexpected information. 254pp. 5⅜ × 8½. 20758-7 Pa. $4.95

THE RED THUMB MARK, R. Austin Freeman. In this first Dr. Thorndyke case, the great scientific detective draws fascinating conclusions from the nature of a single fingerprint. Exciting story, authentic science. 320pp. 5⅜ × 8½. (Available in U.S. only) 25210-8 Pa. $5.95

AN EGYPTIAN HIEROGLYPHIC DICTIONARY, E. A. Wallis Budge. Monumental work containing about 25,000 words or terms that occur in texts ranging from 3000 B.C. to 600 A.D. Each entry consists of a transliteration of the word, the word in hieroglyphs, and the meaning in English. 1,314pp. 6⅜ × 10.
23615-3, 23616-1 Pa., Two-vol. set $27.90

THE COMPLEAT STRATEGYST: Being a Primer on the Theory of Games of Strategy, J. D. Williams. Highly entertaining classic describes, with many illustrated examples, how to select best strategies in conflict situations. Prefaces. Appendices. xvi + 268pp. 5⅜ × 8½. 25101-2 Pa. $5.95

THE ROAD TO OZ, L. Frank Baum. Dorothy meets the Shaggy Man, little Button-Bright and the Rainbow's beautiful daughter in this delightful trip to the magical Land of Oz. 272pp. 5⅜ × 8. 25208-6 Pa. $4.95

POINT AND LINE TO PLANE, Wassily Kandinsky. Seminal exposition of role of point, line, other elements in non-objective painting. Essential to understanding 20th-century art. 127 illustrations. 192pp. 6½ × 9¼. 23808-3 Pa. $4.50

LADY ANNA, Anthony Trollope. Moving chronicle of Countess Lovel's bitter struggle to win for herself and daughter Anna their rightful rank and fortune—perhaps at cost of sanity itself. 384pp. 5⅜ × 8½. 24669-8 Pa. $6.95

EGYPTIAN MAGIC, E. A. Wallis Budge. Sums up all that is known about magic in Ancient Egypt: the role of magic in controlling the gods, powerful amulets that warded off evil spirits, scarabs of immortality, use of wax images, formulas and spells, the secret name, much more. 253pp. 5⅜ × 8½. 22681-6 Pa. $4.00

THE DANCE OF SIVA, Ananda Coomaraswamy. Preeminent authority unfolds the vast metaphysic of India: the revelation of her art, conception of the universe, social organization, etc. 27 reproductions of art masterpieces. 192pp. 5⅜ × 8½.
24817-8 Pa. $5.95

CHRISTMAS CUSTOMS AND TRADITIONS, Clement A. Miles. Origin, evolution, significance of religious, secular practices. Caroling, gifts, yule logs, much more. Full, scholarly yet fascinating; non-sectarian. 400pp. 5⅜ × 8½.
23354-5 Pa. $6.50

THE HUMAN FIGURE IN MOTION, Eadweard Muybridge. More than 4,500 stopped-action photos, in action series, showing undraped men, women, children jumping, lying down, throwing, sitting, wrestling, carrying, etc. 390pp. 7⅞ × 10⅝.
20204-6 Cloth. $21.95

THE MAN WHO WAS THURSDAY, Gilbert Keith Chesterton. Witty, fast-paced novel about a club of anarchists in turn-of-the-century London. Brilliant social, religious, philosophical speculations. 128pp. 5⅜ × 8½. 25121-7 Pa. $3.95

A CEZANNE SKETCHBOOK: Figures, Portraits, Landscapes and Still Lifes, Paul Cezanne. Great artist experiments with tonal effects, light, mass, other qualities in over 100 drawings. A revealing view of developing master painter, precursor of Cubism. 102 black-and-white illustrations. 144pp. 8¾ × 6⅜. 24790-2 Pa. $5.95

AN ENCYCLOPEDIA OF BATTLES: Accounts of Over 1,560 Battles from 1479 B.C. to the Present, David Eggenberger. Presents essential details of every major battle in recorded history, from the first battle of Megiddo in 1479 B.C. to Grenada in 1984. List of Battle Maps. New Appendix covering the years 1967–1984. Index. 99 illustrations. 544pp. 6½ × 9¼. 24913-1 Pa. $14.95

AN ETYMOLOGICAL DICTIONARY OF MODERN ENGLISH, Ernest Weekley. Richest, fullest work, by foremost British lexicographer. Detailed word histories. Inexhaustible. Total of 856pp. 6½ × 9¼.
21873-2, 21874-0 Pa., Two-vol. set $17.00

WEBSTER'S AMERICAN MILITARY BIOGRAPHIES, edited by Robert McHenry. Over 1,000 figures who shaped 3 centuries of American military history. Detailed biographies of Nathan Hale, Douglas MacArthur, Mary Hallaren, others. Chronologies of engagements, more. Introduction. Addenda. 1,033 entries in alphabetical order. xi + 548pp. 6½ × 9¼. (Available in U.S. only)
24758-9 Pa. $11.95

LIFE IN ANCIENT EGYPT, Adolf Erman. Detailed older account, with much not in more recent books: domestic life, religion, magic, medicine, commerce, and whatever else needed for complete picture. Many illustrations. 597pp. 5⅜ × 8½.
22632-8 Pa. $8.50

HISTORIC COSTUME IN PICTURES, Braun & Schneider. Over 1,450 costumed figures shown, covering a wide variety of peoples: kings, emperors, nobles, priests, servants, soldiers, scholars, townsfolk, peasants, merchants, courtiers, cavaliers, and more. 256pp. 8⅜ × 11¼. 23150-X Pa. $7.95

THE NOTEBOOKS OF LEONARDO DA VINCI, edited by J. P. Richter. Extracts from manuscripts reveal great genius; on painting, sculpture, anatomy, sciences, geography, etc. Both Italian and English. 186 ms. pages reproduced, plus 500 additional drawings, including studies for *Last Supper, Sforza* monument, etc. 860pp. 7⅞ × 10¾. (Available in U.S. only) 22572-0, 22573-9 Pa., Two-vol. set $25.90

THE ART NOUVEAU STYLE BOOK OF ALPHONSE MUCHA: All 72 Plates from "Documents Decoratifs" in Original Color, Alphonse Mucha. Rare copyright-free design portfolio by high priest of Art Nouveau. Jewelry, wallpaper, stained glass, furniture, figure studies, plant and animal motifs, etc. Only complete one-volume edition. 80pp. 9⅜ × 12¼. 24044-4 Pa. $8.95

ANIMALS: 1,419 COPYRIGHT-FREE ILLUSTRATIONS OF MAMMALS, BIRDS, FISH, INSECTS, ETC., edited by Jim Harter. Clear wood engravings present, in extremely lifelike poses, over 1,000 species of animals. One of the most extensive pictorial sourcebooks of its kind. Captions. Index. 284pp. 9 × 12.
23766-4 Pa. $9.95

OBELISTS FLY HIGH, C. Daly King. Masterpiece of American detective fiction, long out of print, involves murder on a 1935 transcontinental flight—"a very thrilling story"—NY Times. Unabridged and unaltered republication of the edition published by William Collins Sons & Co. Ltd., London, 1935. 288pp. 5⅜ × 8½. (Available in U.S. only) 25036-9 Pa. $4.95

VICTORIAN AND EDWARDIAN FASHION: A Photographic Survey, Alison Gernsheim. First fashion history completely illustrated by contemporary photographs. Full text plus 235 photos, 1840–1914, in which many celebrities appear. 240pp. 6½ × 9¼. 24205-6 Pa. $6.00

THE ART OF THE FRENCH ILLUSTRATED BOOK, 1700–1914, Gordon N. Ray. Over 630 superb book illustrations by Fragonard, Delacroix, Daumier, Doré, Grandville, Manet, Mucha, Steinlen, Toulouse-Lautrec and many others. Preface. Introduction. 633 halftones. Indices of artists, authors & titles, binders and provenances. Appendices. Bibliography. 608pp. 8⅜ × 11¼. 25086-5 Pa. $24.95

THE WONDERFUL WIZARD OF OZ, L. Frank Baum. Facsimile in full color of America's finest children's classic. 143 illustrations by W. W. Denslow. 267pp. 5⅜ × 8½. 20691-2 Pa. $5.95

FRONTIERS OF MODERN PHYSICS: New Perspectives on Cosmology, Relativity, Black Holes and Extraterrestrial Intelligence, Tony Rothman, et al. For the intelligent layman. Subjects include: cosmological models of the universe; black holes; the neutrino; the search for extraterrestrial intelligence. Introduction. 46 black-and-white illustrations. 192pp. 5⅜ × 8½. 24587-X Pa. $6.95

THE FRIENDLY STARS, Martha Evans Martin & Donald Howard Menzel. Classic text marshalls the stars together in an engaging, non-technical survey, presenting them as sources of beauty in night sky. 23 illustrations. Foreword. 2 star charts. Index. 147pp. 5⅜ × 8½. 21099-5 Pa. $3.50

FADS AND FALLACIES IN THE NAME OF SCIENCE, Martin Gardner. Fair, witty appraisal of cranks, quacks, and quackeries of science and pseudoscience: hollow earth, Velikovsky, orgone energy, Dianetics, flying saucers, Bridey Murphy, food and medical fads, etc. Revised, expanded In the Name of Science. "A very able and even-tempered presentation."—The New Yorker. 363pp. 5⅜ × 8.
20394-8 Pa. $6.50

ANCIENT EGYPT: ITS CULTURE AND HISTORY, J. E Manchip White. From pre-dynastics through Ptolemies: society, history, political structure, religion, daily life, literature, cultural heritage. 48 plates. 217pp. 5⅜ × 8½. 22548-8 Pa. $4.95

SIR HARRY HOTSPUR OF HUMBLETHWAITE, Anthony Trollope. Incisive, unconventional psychological study of a conflict between a wealthy baronet, his idealistic daughter, and their scapegrace cousin. The 1870 novel in its first inexpensive edition in years. 250pp. 5⅜ × 8½. 24953-0 Pa. $5.95

LASERS AND HOLOGRAPHY, Winston E. Kock. Sound introduction to burgeoning field, expanded (1981) for second edition. Wave patterns, coherence, lasers, diffraction, zone plates, properties of holograms, recent advances. 84 illustrations. 160pp. 5⅜ × 8¼. (Except in United Kingdom) 24041-X Pa. $3.50

INTRODUCTION TO ARTIFICIAL INTELLIGENCE: SECOND, EN-LARGED EDITION, Philip C. Jackson, Jr. Comprehensive survey of artificial intelligence—the study of how machines (computers) can be made to act intelligently. Includes introductory and advanced material. Extensive notes updating the main text. 132 black-and-white illustrations. 512pp. 5⅜ × 8½. 24864-X Pa. $8.95

HISTORY OF INDIAN AND INDONESIAN ART, Ananda K. Coomaraswamy. Over 400 illustrations illuminate classic study of Indian art from earliest Harappa finds to early 20th century. Provides philosophical, religious and social insights. 304pp. 6⅛ × 9⅜. 25005-9 Pa. $8.95

THE GOLEM, Gustav Meyrink. Most famous supernatural novel in modern European literature, set in Ghetto of Old Prague around 1890. Compelling story of mystical experiences, strange transformations, profound terror. 13 black-and-white illustrations. 224pp. 5⅜ × 8½. (Available in U.S. only) 25025-3 Pa. $5.95

ARMADALE, Wilkie Collins. Third great mystery novel by the author of *The Woman in White* and *The Moonstone*. Original magazine version with 40 illustrations. 597pp. 5⅜ × 8½. 23429-0 Pa. $9.95

PICTORIAL ENCYCLOPEDIA OF HISTORIC ARCHITECTURAL PLANS, DETAILS AND ELEMENTS: With 1,880 Line Drawings of Arches, Domes, Doorways, Facades, Gables, Windows, etc., John Theodore Haneman. Sourcebook of inspiration for architects, designers, others. Bibliography. Captions. 141pp. 9 × 12. 24605-1 Pa. $6.95

BENCHLEY LOST AND FOUND, Robert Benchley. Finest humor from early 30's, about pet peeves, child psychologists, post office and others. Mostly unavailable elsewhere. 73 illustrations by Peter Arno and others. 183pp. 5⅜ × 8½. 22410-4 Pa. $3.95

ERTÉ GRAPHICS, Erté. Collection of striking color graphics: *Seasons, Alphabet, Numerals, Aces* and *Precious Stones*. 50 plates, including 4 on covers. 48pp. 9⅜ × 12¼. 23580-7 Pa. $6.95

THE JOURNAL OF HENRY D. THOREAU, edited by Bradford Torrey, F. H. Allen. Complete reprinting of 14 volumes, 1837–61, over two million words; the sourcebooks for *Walden*, etc. Definitive. All original sketches, plus 75 photographs. 1,804pp. 8½ × 12¼. 20312-3, 20313-1 Cloth., Two-vol. set $80.00

CASTLES: THEIR CONSTRUCTION AND HISTORY, Sidney Toy. Traces castle development from ancient roots. Nearly 200 photographs and drawings illustrate moats, keeps, baileys, many other features. Caernarvon, Dover Castles, Hadrian's Wall, Tower of London, dozens more. 256pp. 5⅜ × 8¼. 24898-4 Pa. $5.95

AMERICAN CLIPPER SHIPS: 1833-1858, Octavius T. Howe & Frederick C. Matthews. Fully-illustrated, encyclopedic review of 352 clipper ships from the period of America's greatest maritime supremacy. Introduction. 109 halftones. 5 black-and-white line illustrations. Index. Total of 928pp. 5⅜ × 8½.
25115-2, 25116-0 Pa., Two vol. set $17.90

TOWARDS A NEW ARCHITECTURE, Le Corbusier. Pioneering manifesto by great architect, near legendary founder of "International School." Technical and aesthetic theories, views on industry, economics, relation of form to function, "mass-production spirit," much more. Profusely illustrated. Unabridged translation of 13th French edition. Introduction by Frederick Etchells. 320pp. 6⅛ × 9¼. (Available in U.S. only)
25023-7 Pa. $8.95

THE BOOK OF KELLS, edited by Blanche Cirker. Inexpensive collection of 32 full-color, full-page plates from the greatest illuminated manuscript of the Middle Ages, painstakingly reproduced from rare facsimile edition. Publisher's Note. Captions. 32pp. 9⅜ × 12¼.
24345-1 Pa. $4.95

BEST SCIENCE FICTION STORIES OF H. G. WELLS, H. G. Wells. Full novel *The Invisible Man*, plus 17 short stories: "The Crystal Egg," "Aepyornis Island," "The Strange Orchid," etc. 303pp. 5⅜ × 8½. (Available in U.S. only)
21531-8 Pa. $4.95

AMERICAN SAILING SHIPS: Their Plans and History, Charles G. Davis. Photos, construction details of schooners, frigates, clippers, other sailcraft of 18th to early 20th centuries—plus entertaining discourse on design, rigging, nautical lore, much more. 137 black-and-white illustrations. 240pp. 6⅛ × 9¼.
24658-2 Pa. $5.95

ENTERTAINING MATHEMATICAL PUZZLES, Martin Gardner. Selection of author's favorite conundrums involving arithmetic, money, speed, etc., with lively commentary. Complete solutions. 112pp. 5⅜ × 8½.
25211-6 Pa. $2.95

THE WILL TO BELIEVE, HUMAN IMMORTALITY, William James. Two books bound together. Effect of irrational on logical, and arguments for human immortality. 402pp. 5⅜ × 8½.
20291-7 Pa. $7.50

THE HAUNTED MONASTERY and THE CHINESE MAZE MURDERS, Robert Van Gulik. 2 full novels by Van Gulik continue adventures of Judge Dee and his companions. An evil Taoist monastery, seemingly supernatural events; overgrown topiary maze that hides strange crimes. Set in 7th-century China. 27 illustrations. 328pp. 5⅜ × 8½.
23502-5 Pa. $5.95

CELEBRATED CASES OF JUDGE DEE (DEE GOONG AN), translated by Robert Van Gulik. Authentic 18th-century Chinese detective novel; Dee and associates solve three interlocked cases. Led to Van Gulik's own stories with same characters. Extensive introduction. 9 illustrations. 237pp. 5⅜ × 8½.
23337-5 Pa. $4.95

Prices subject to change without notice.